"WHEN I STARTED TEACHING,
I WISH I HAD KNOWN..."

This book is dedicated to

Sean Duarte, a beginning teacher extraordinaire.

"WHEN I STARTED TEACHING, I WISH I HAD KNOWN..."

Weekly Wisdom for Beginning Teachers

36 Weeks
of Wisdom,
Advice, &
Support

CAROL PELLETIER RADFORD

CORWIN

FOR INFORMATION:

Corwin

A SAGE Company

2455 Teller Road

Thousand Oaks, California 91320

(800) 233-9936

www.corwin.com

SAGE Publications Ltd.

1 Oliver's Yard

55 City Road

London EC1Y 1SP

United Kingdom

SAGE Publications India Pvt. Ltd.

Unit No 323-333, Third Floor, F-Block

International Trade Tower Nehru Place

New Delhi 110 019

SAGE Publications Asia-Pacific Pte. Ltd.

18 Cross Street #10-10/11/12

China Square Central

Singapore 048423

President: Mike Soules

Vice President and Editorial
  Director: Monica Eckman

Director and Publisher,
  Corwin Classroom: Lisa Luedeke

Associate Content
  Development Editor: Sarah Ross

Project Editor: Amy Schroller

Copy Editor: Karen E. Taylor

Typesetter: C&M Digitals (P) Ltd.

Proofreader: Theresa Kay

Cover Designer: Gail Buschman

Marketing Manager: Megan Naidl

Art images on the title page and section-opening pages are the creations of the author, Carol Pelletier Radford.

Printed in the United Kingdom

Library of Congress Control Number: 2023936033

This book is printed on acid-free paper.

23 24 25 26 27 10 9 8 7 6 5 4 3 2 1

CONTENTS

CLOSING THE SCHOOL YEAR WITH INTENTION ~ CELEBRATE YOUR GROWTH   139

LOOKING BACK, LOOKING FORWARD ~ REFLECT AND PLAN   164

Appendices

For resources related to *"When I Started Teaching,*
I Wish I Had Known . . ."
visit the companion website at
resources.corwin.com/WeeklyWisdom.

LETTER TO BEGINNING TEACHERS

Dear Beginning Teachers,

This is a book of wisdom from experienced teachers who have come before you. Our wisdom is offered to you as a gift to support your growth and enhance your success in the classroom. We all know that learning how to teach takes many years. It also requires us to pay attention to the ways in which we manage our time, our classrooms, our students, and our own self-care.

One of my mentors, Roland S. Barth, wrote a book titled *Improving Schools From Within: Teachers, Parents, and Principals Can Make the Difference.* This book profoundly influenced my perspective on my role as a teacher. Not only did it inspire me to share ideas, reach out for help when I needed it, and eventually become a teacher leader, but it also made me feel important. It made me realize I could make decisions and improve the school from my classroom.

As educators, we often get advice from people who are *outside* of our classrooms. What we need today is advice and wisdom from other teachers who have been *inside* the classroom. This is where the true wisdom of our profession lives.

> *The most powerful form of learning, the most sophisticated form of staff development, comes not from listening to the good words of others but from sharing what we know with others. . . .*
>
> *By reflecting on what we do, by giving it coherence, and by sharing and articulating our craft knowledge, we make meaning and learn.*

~ Roland S. Barth (1986)

It has been a great honor to read the stories, the practical tips, and the self-care advice from the experienced teachers who graciously submitted their wisdom to this book. Their craft knowledge demonstrates how much we know and how much is hidden from us if we don't share our ideas with each other.

Stay connected to your heart, and remember why you chose this profession.

Carol

"When I Started Teaching, I Wish I Had Known . . ."

ACKNOWLEDGMENTS

Special thanks to you, Lisa Luedeke, for sharing your vision for this book and inviting me to write it.

Thank you to all the teachers who contributed to this book and the companion website, and who took the time to share their stories. Your courage and authentic voice offer our next generation of teachers the wisdom they need to succeed.

I would not be where I am today without the support of my Mentoring in Action team: Karen DeRusha, Karen Gannon, Shonna Ryan, Heather Hollins, Joanne Koch, Joanne Mendes, Kathi Rogers, and Kathy Gagne. You embody the ideal of paying it forward. We will continue to share our enthusiasm for the education profession.

Thank you, David, for generously taking on most of the household duties so I could gather the stories, create the overall message, and write this book.

Mike and Adam, I could not be prouder to see you both choose teaching as your career. Your students are so lucky to have you as teachers.

I am grateful to all my students over the years who have shared their stories and dreams with me. You have been my greatest teachers.

ABOUT THE AUTHOR

Carol Pelletier Radford is the founder of Mentoring in Action, an organization dedicated to supporting beginning teachers and their mentors. She is an experienced teacher, university administrator, and certified yoga instructor. Carol received her education doctorate at the Harvard Graduate School of Education where she focused her studies on mentoring and teacher leadership. You can find her on the beach in Falmouth, Massachusetts or Venice, Florida. Her sweetest dream was to write this book!

Website: https://mentoringinaction.com/

Twitter: @MentorinAction

Facebook: @MentoringinAction4Teachers

Instagram: @cpradford

WISDOM HELPS YOU GROW

Wis-dom: noun ~ the quality of having experience, knowledge, and good judgment; the quality of being wise. "Listen to their words of wisdom."

Teacher wisdom comes from actual experience in the classroom. It is an intangible quality gained through life experience or, in this case, teaching experience. When we look at the data that report teachers make at least 1,500 decisions each day (Klein, 2021), we realize how important these responses are to success in the classroom. A wise teacher is one with good sense and an attitude that has evolved through much experience. You will meet some of these wise teachers in this book—teachers from all subject areas and levels and with varying years in the profession who have learned from experience and want to share it with you. These teachers are your mentors for this year, providing you with guidance from their inside-the-classroom experiences, and wisdom learned from the mistakes they have made.

Beginning teachers are often very surprised by the quick pace of the classroom and how to respond to the many decisions they make in every moment of the day. When students walk through that classroom door the environment quickly changes. Novice teachers need practical ways to manage their time, their classroom routines, and the students' energy, so the classroom doesn't turn into chaos. The old paradigm of preparing teachers to learn how to teach in a trial-by-fire experience is not helpful to you or your students. Our goal is to support your growth and development by sharing our wisdom through stories, practical tips, and advice for self-care. Why reinvent the wheel when you can be mentored by experienced, wise teachers?

Needs of Beginning Teachers

As a beginner, you probably have come to understand that your competence in your subject area is not always enough to engage your students and make you successful in the classroom. You may have some level of confidence, but you are still looking around at those experienced teachers and wondering, How did she do that? What is the *magic* experienced teachers have that you can't seem to grasp? You may even have asked yourself, How can I find this intangible wisdom?

Educators around the world are coming to realize that competence and confidence are not enough to keep beginning teachers teaching. Retention of beginning teachers is a problem. We are all now realizing that we must have an intentional focus on teacher wellness if we want our novices to succeed in the classroom. As a beginner, you may be overwhelmed by the workload, the day-to-day rhythm of teaching, and those 1,500 decisions you have to make. I have learned that when we work harder and longer hours it influences our health, and it actually doesn't help us maintain our balance in the classroom. That is why we include a "Take Care of You" piece of wisdom each week. Your health and wellness influence the classroom environment.

In addition to taking your own wellness seriously, as a beginning teacher, you want to learn more about how to manage your classroom more effectively. How you manage your time, your energy, all those classroom routines, and any student behavior issue is important to creating a smoothly running classroom. That is why we include a piece of practical wisdom in one of these management areas each week.

Growth and development require all the right conditions. Sun, water, good soil, and conditions for reaching up and taking risks. Teaching is a creative pursuit. Teachers are not only technicians to deliver content knowledge; they are also inspiring role models and creators. YOU are important.

Wisdom Through Stories

The stories you will read in this book each week are shared by teachers of varied ages; from different subject areas, states, and districts; and with various years of experience. Some are still teaching, and others have retired. I refer to retired teachers who are still inspired as *legacy teachers*. Their wisdom and dedication to manifesting a fulfilling career in teaching are inspiring. Each teacher was invited to share a significant experience that they recalled from their teaching career that helped them develop as a teacher.

I believe teacher stories are important. I know when I have shared my stories with teachers in the past, they felt the message and used it to reflect on their own experiences. You have stories too. Use this book's prompts at the end of each week to jot down your insights. Sharing our stories with each other is what creates our "community of teacher learners," and it helps us know we are part of something bigger than our school and district. We are part of a noble profession of educators.

I would like to share one of my stories with you. It is titled "Bloom Where You're Planted" and is adapted from *Teaching With Light: Ten Lessons for Finding Wisdom, Balance, and Inspiration* (2021).

My school burned to the ground the year I was accepted into a teaching sabbatical. My classroom was destroyed, and my school was gone. Everything I had created for my elementary classroom was lost. I had to fulfill my obligation to a fellowship I'd been offered, all the while knowing at the end of the year I had to return to my teaching position, whatever that would be. It was an awkward time for me personally and professionally. When I returned, I was one of two teachers assigned to teach in one of the portable classrooms parked in the back of the school. My old classroom had colorful learning centers, rugs, special decorations, and personal items for the students. This portable had nothing, except some old desks that hadn't been used in decades. I was devastated. I remember crying on the first day of school as I looked at the trailer. I was going through the grieving process that my colleagues had experienced the year before. Only I was doing it alone.

I felt like a first-year teacher—isolated and overwhelmed. I reached out to my colleague Pat from the fellowship and talked about leaving teaching. I didn't think I could recreate all I had done in my classroom and do it in a trailer! Pat came to visit me.

I sobbed. She listened. As she left, she handed me a card with the message *Bloom where you're planted* on the front. She encouraged me to stay put and not make a hasty decision to change my teaching assignment, reminding me, "You bring your skills, your years of teaching experience, and your passion for teaching to this moment. Use your strengths."

One of my proudest moments as a teacher happened that year. A student named Billy was waving furiously, trying to get my attention one day near the end of the year. He was shouting, "I finished my book! I did it! I finished the whole book!" Tears came to my eyes as I thought about this student. He was in the fifth grade, and he had been able to hide for all these years that he couldn't read. I noticed this deficit one day. Instead of pointing it out to him or asking him about it, we began to read together every day. And then, one day, he could read on his own. Years later I reconnected with Billy, and he shared his memory of learning to read and how he went on to college and became a teacher!

The crisis of losing my classroom to fire, being placed in a portable trailer in the back of the school, and feeling isolated for a year could have led me to leave teaching or look for another position. Instead, it was the year I learned most about who I was as a teacher. I not only bloomed as a teacher but was able to help one of my students bloom, too. I learned I really was a good teacher, and a good teacher can teach anywhere.

How to Use This Book

The obvious way to use this book is to read each week's entry in order and reflect on its wisdom to see how it relates to your growth as a teacher. But if you are anything like me, you might want to skip to the end and peek to see what is ahead for you. You may even want to read all of the management ideas sprinkled throughout the book because that is what you need right now.

This is your book of wisdom, and you can use it the way that best supports you. What I do highly recommend is that you schedule your *Weekly Wisdom* into your regular weekly planning time. You want time to read and reflect on what might be useful to you each week. I also encourage you to review the bios and photos of each teacher on the companion website to acknowledge their contribution to your journey.

HOW WEEKLY WISDOM IS ORGANIZED

School years have cycles and rhythms that relate to activities or content knowledge to be taught. I like to think of them as seasons. This book is organized into weeks and grouped into sections by seasons. These are not strict boundaries by any means—just a way to think about the wisdom in an organized way through the cycle of a school year.

Weeks 1–8

Getting Started ~ Create a Community of Learners

Weeks 9–16

Gaining Momentum ~ Find Your Strengths

"When I Started Teaching, I Wish I Had Known . . ."

Weeks 17–30

Staying in the Flow ~ Focus on Teaching and Learning

Weeks 31–36

Closing the School Year With Intention ~ Celebrate Your Growth

WHAT TO EXPECT EACH WEEK

Within each week, you will find four types of wisdom from a featured teacher to take in, explore, and practice: a story, a management tip, a self-care message, and an affirmation.

The Story

As you read the stories, I invite you to be open to the big ideas the teacher is sharing. It doesn't matter if it is not about your age group or subject area. Listen for the key message: how this teacher learned how to be successful. In my story above, a key message was this: *You bring your skills, your years of teaching experience, and your passion for teaching to this moment. Use your strengths.*

After you read each story, you will have an opportunity to "Pause. Reflect. Act." This is a signal for you to use your insight and your wisdom to think about how this message is useful to you. You may want to keep a journal or use the journal on the companion website to jot down your thoughts. This writing will be useful to you at the end of the year when you look back to see how much you have grown.

The Management Tip

This is where you will find practical wisdom for the classroom. The research says that most teachers say they need to know a lot more about MANAGEMENT! Time management, classroom routines and rituals, and ways to manage student behavior issues. So, each week you will read the teacher's suggestion for you in one of those three management areas. Here is an example:

How to Manage Student Papers

Here is one of my best time management tips for collecting assignments from students. Assign a number to each student in my classroom. The number relates to the alphabetical order of students in my grade book. Before students pass in any written assignment, they put their "number" in the upper right corner along with their name. A student leader collects the papers and puts them in numerical order for me, so I can easily enter the completed assignment in my grade book. If a number is missing, we can see if that student is absent or just forgot to hand in the assignment. A sticky note on the top sheet lists any missing numbers for easy follow-up with students when they return to school. It's an easy and efficient way to collect papers, record grades quickly, and see which students were absent.

The Self-Care Message

Featured teachers will also share how they take time for themselves so that school doesn't become so overwhelming. You may already do some of these things, and some ideas may be new to you. The message is for you to do something that resonates with you. The goal is for you to find ways outside of schoolwork to live and enjoy. Many of us "love" being teachers and find that working more and harder is just what we do. But we all know that is a recipe for disaster when the challenges get more intense and we don't have a regular routine in place for detaching from school. Here is an example:

Walk in Nature

One of my favorite activities to calm myself down is to take a forest-bathing walk. The term *forest bathing*, known as *shinrin-yoku* in Japan, is a way to find peace and lower anxiety. I dedicate a specified amount of time to be on a nature path near my home. The goal is not exercise but to take in the sights, sounds, and smells of the forest through our senses. Forest therapy works for me to relax my nervous system and quiet my mind. It is best done alone, but if a friend wants to join in, remember there is no talking. It is a meditation-in-motion activity.

The Affirmation

Positive self-talk can take the form of affirmations. These are positive phrases or statements we use to stay in the moment and keep us from any negative or unhelpful thoughts. They are easy to use and offer us a way to stay focused on the positive. I have included one each week, drawing on the content of the teacher's story and message. All you need to do is repeat it or write it in your journal to help turn your week around. We often get caught up in what we can't do, and the struggles sometimes dominate. Using some positive self-talk can make a difference. And yes, this is based in science—and research shows it works if you practice.

Sample Affirmations for Teachers

Who I am is enough.

I am guided by inner wisdom.

I express my truth with confidence.

Energy fills my life.

I am free to express what I'm feeling.

I know the right thing to do.

Use the affirmations in each *Weekly Wisdom* entry to bring a positive focus to your week.

Stay Inspired

You will notice common themes emerge from the stories and practical wisdom. Paying attention to your students, keeping lists, and unplugging from the work will be shared by many of these experienced teachers. When you see the same message repeated, note it as a reminder to look at this topic again more deeply. We don't learn how to teach in one year, or two, or even twenty! Teaching is an ongoing development—we continue to grow, learn, and emerge as the most important influencers of our students' success.

Remember, you are not alone. You can reach out at any time to an experienced teacher in your school or call a friend. Find a mentor if you don't have one. Don't let your stress overwhelm you. Learn how to find that balance in your home and work life, so you can find ways to enjoy teaching.

We know that this one little book of wisdom may not be enough for you and that you may need more support to find the momentum you seek. This is just a beginning step. Use *Weekly Wisdom* as a nurturing guide, and let this wisdom from these mentor teachers support you so you can ease through your beginning years gracefully. Nourish yourself and be kind to yourself. *You* are what your students need most.

This is your book, your journey, and your year. Read the stories, reflect on the wisdom shared, and take away what resonates with you, and what works for your classroom. You get to decide how you will integrate the ideas into your busy life one week at a time. And remember, *YOU* bring *your* wisdom and intuitive self to the classroom too. Listen to your gut and use your own intuition to guide your decisions.

Most of all, have some fun! Teaching has some hilarious moments that you just can't make up. Let's not miss the joy because all of our attention is on the challenges. Your health and wellness influence your students' health and wellness. In many ways, this book is as much about your students as it is about you. As one teacher said to me, "Happy Healthy Teachers = Happy Healthy Students."

Welcome to your *Weekly Wisdom* journey. Let's begin!

GETTING STARTED
CREATE A COMMUNITY OF LEARNERS
(WEEKS 1–8)

The beginning of the school year can be quite hectic. Preparing for those first weeks of school directly influences how you will kick off your school year. During these eight weeks, it is really important to focus on getting to know your students and creating the routines that you will use all year long. To create a community of learners you need to focus on your students' needs and how you will present yourself to them.

The experienced teachers in this section will share their stories, their mistakes, what they learned, and how they have changed their practices to be more compassionate teachers.

Schedule time each week to read and reflect on what is most useful to you and write your insights in a personal journal or use the online option on the companion website. (Visit the companion website at **resources.corwin.com/WeeklyWisdom**.)

1

GIVE STUDENTS
A FRESH START

Meaghan Calkins
9 years

Since my first year of teaching, I have taught high school freshmen. I was told, "This class coming is just awful!" I decided my very first year that I was not going to listen to the opinions about the upcoming freshmen, and I was going to give every student a clean slate and a new start.

I tell each one of my freshmen classes this, and I believe it resonates with the students as an opportunity to truly become who they want to be perceived as. I learned very early on that there are truly no "bad" students; they are just kids trying to do the best they can given circumstances they had zero say in. In short, I realized my own professional affirmation: If you can get a student to trust you, then you can get that student to do anything!

I give every student a clean
slate and a new start.

Practical Wisdom for the Classroom

Consistency, consistency, consistency! I cannot express enough that any classroom policy or expectation you state during the first couple days of school must be upheld all year long. Idle threats will get you nowhere. Gray areas of classroom management will confuse students. Create fair routines and procedures, and if you do have to change them, explain why.

Take Care of You

In my first year of teaching I was full of motivation and eager to "change the world one student at a time!" I soon realized that before I can help someone else, I need to make sure I am taking care of myself first. To a novice teacher, I would say there must be a point in the day when you unplug from work. You will never feel like you have "completed everything." Therefore, now is the time to learn to keep your health and well-being a priority—before you experience teacher burnout early in your career. Make every effort to maintain any healthy habits that you had prior to becoming a teacher. For example, if you exercise in the morning, keep exercising in the morning. If you read the paper and enjoy a cup of coffee in the morning, continue to do that. Do not work 24/7.

PAUSE. REFLECT. ACT.

Hearing that an entire class is "awful" can be a daunting message to a new teacher.

- How will you share your positive view of your students' potential with them?
- What will you do this week to support your growth as a teacher?
- What will you keep doing that is good for you?

Write your responses to the prompts in a journal to further your reflection and to help you remember what you are learning. An online journal for your use is available on our companion website (resources.corwin.com/WeeklyWisdom). ●

REFLECTIONS

MAKE STUDENT
CONFIDENCE YOUR GOAL

Jessica Concha
4 years

One of the biggest lessons I have learned in my career is the value of nurturing your relationships with all of your students. Every year, you will have a variety of personalities in your classroom. Some students will naturally participate, engage in class discussion, and share about their personal lives. Other students may not feel comfortable doing such things. Thus, it can be easy for more introverted students to feel overshadowed or unnoticed. Further, because these students are less likely to approach you on their own, it is critical that you as the teacher set out to develop your relationship with them and continually seek opportunities for their personal growth. I made it my mission to seek out students that struggle with communicating with others and with speaking up during class discussions.

I once had a student with autism who was very afraid to engage in conversation with her peers or to interact with her teachers. I made it my goal to find ways to gradually increase her confidence in communicating with others.

Early in the school year, we set a goal for her to raise her hand at least two times during the day. At the start, before asking a question, I would tap on her desk two times to warn her that I was going to call on her (a strategy my co-teacher recommended). She would then know to raise her hand when I asked the question, and I would call on her.

As time progressed, her confidence in engaging in class discussion grew exponentially. One afternoon, I took time to pull her aside to let her know how proud I was of her progress in participating in class and stepping outside of her comfort zone.

I told her that I wanted to send a letter home or make a call to her parents to express how delighted I was in her growth. Her beaming smile is an image I will never forget, and a constant reminder of the importance of lovingly pushing students to achieve their full potential. Since then, she raises her hand voluntarily, asks to come up to the board, and is genuinely excited to share her thoughts with the class.

My experience with this student taught me not to become discouraged if I didn't see results right away. I also learned the importance of consistently pushing students toward achieving their goals—even if they become frustrated or lack motivation or confidence.

Beginning teachers should set out to identify opportunities for personal growth in each of their students, even those with whom it may be difficult to form a relationship. It is very easy to get caught up in students' grades and perfect scores. However, throughout my career, I have observed personal and social growth can dramatically influence academic success. Your students are with you every day—be sure to invest in them emotionally, not just academically!

Her beaming smile is an image I will never forget, and a constant reminder of the importance of lovingly pushing students to achieve their full potential.

Practical Wisdom for the Classroom

I have learned that there is no benefit in interrupting class to discipline a student. If anything, it gives the student more attention, and sometimes students act out for that very reason. If you have a student misbehaving, find ways you can communicate that the student needs to make a change in behavior or work effort, without relying only on verbal discipline. Talk to students individually and quietly at their desks and remind them of your expectations and be sure to be at eye level when you are speaking to them. You can also establish nonverbal cues to communicate that they need to adjust their behavior.

Take Care of You

Managing your time during the school day is key to avoiding burnout and stopping work from interfering with your personal life. Be sure to maximize the time you have blocked off to create or review lesson plans, grades, etc., to avoid having to complete those tasks at home. It is important to make time for the things you enjoy—not only on the weekends but also during the week.

●●● **I GIVE MYSELF PERMISSION TO LOG OFF AT THE END OF THE DAY.**

PAUSE. REFLECT. ACT.

Jessica's message about helping students be more confident is important to your role as a teacher.

- How will you interact with students who may not be on task?
- How will you schedule your free time?
- What will you do this week to support your growth as a teacher?

Write your responses to the prompts in a journal to further your reflection and to help you remember what you are learning. An online journal for your use is available on our companion website (resources.corwin.com/WeeklyWisdom). ●

3

CREATE ROUTINES FOR EVERYTHING

Linda Howard
30 years

As a beginning teacher, you will often feel overwhelmed. If you have opportunities, especially during your practicum, observe a variety of classrooms. You will take the best from each teacher and create a learning environment that works for everyone. Prioritize your time by making decisions about what's important for you to focus on in the classroom. One BIG thing I learned in my career as a teacher is that students come first. Everything else is just stuff.

This goal helped me to filter out situations that were out of my control and to keep focus on my students. It's easy to get wrapped up in day-to-day things that, in the long run, do not improve your quality as a teacher or the learning environment of your classroom. I'm very appreciative of everyone who occasionally reminded me that I'm there first for the kids. It then became a natural part of my teaching and classroom culture.

One BIG thing I learned in my career as a teacher is that students come first. Everything else is just stuff.

Practical Wisdom for the Classroom

The first six weeks of school are very important. Getting-to-know-you activities during the first weeks of school help build a community in the classroom. One activity that I found kids enjoy, and that helps them learn a lot about one another, is a human scavenger hunt. Some examples of what students would ask: Find someone who . . . walks to school, has brothers or sisters, is an only child, likes to swim, and so on. It's a fun activity that gets kids moving and gives them a chance to speak to everyone.

Take Care of You

A group of teacher friends and I, every Wednesday after school, went for a 3-mile jog. It's one of my fondest memories because not only did I get a decent workout, but the camaraderie also grew each week and each year. Plus, it was a great idea-sharing and venting time! It helped take care of both my body and mind.

••• I ENJOY CREATING A COMMUNITY OF LEARNERS.

PAUSE. REFLECT. ACT.

Linda spends a lot of time getting to know her students and having them learn about each other.

- How will you get to know the students in your classroom?

- Why is this time well spent?

- What will you do this week to support your growth as a teacher?

Write your responses to the prompts in a journal to further your reflection and to help you remember what you are learning. An online journal for your use is available on our companion website (resources.corwin.com/WeeklyWisdom). ●

LEARN ABOUT YOUR STUDENTS' FAMILIES

Adam Pelletier
18 years

When I started teaching, I didn't think about the home life of my students. I learned to pay more attention to this when I had several students failing in my class, and I needed to call home to tell the parents. As I prepared for the calls, I reviewed the files in the school office and discovered each of these failing students had a challenging home situation. One lived with her grandparents, one student's file had a note on it that said, "Don't talk to the father," and another file mentioned that this student had to stay home periodically to babysit for siblings while mom worked. This experience gave me a better understanding of what was preventing these students from participating fully in my class. Now, I know that learning about *all* students' lives outside of school helps me to better understand their challenges. After I learned about the family life of these students, I released my judgment about why they were failing my class. It became less about me as their teacher and more about them. Each of these three students had a different family issue that was preventing them from being consistently successful. I learned to modify assignments and talk to students when I noticed them failing. I am glad I discovered this because it has made me a more effective teacher.

I learned to modify assignments and talk to students when I noticed them failing.

Practical Wisdom for the Classroom

One way I create a community of learners in my classroom is to take a photo of each student at the beginning of the school year and invite each student to write a short bio to place next to it. One year I had them write a list of qualities using the letters of their first name, and other years I have had them write about their hobbies, favorite movies, or just anything that they love to do. The students love to read about each other and find out what they have in common.

Take Care of You

Teaching can be all consuming, and it is hard to turn off my mind at the end of the day. One way I shift my focus is to cook. I love to make bread, pizza, and even donuts! It might not be the healthiest hobby, but it sure does taste good, and it takes my mind off school and the problems from the day.

●●● I INTENTIONALLY INTRODUCE MY STUDENTS TO EACH OTHER.

PAUSE. REFLECT. ACT.

Sometimes we don't know why students are failing.

- How does Adam's message inspire you to learn more about your students?
- Review the school records and talk with the students who may be disengaged so as to learn more about their lives outside of school. What did you learn?
- What will you do this week to support your growth as a teacher?

Write your responses to the prompts in a journal to further your reflection and to help you remember what you are learning. An online journal for your use is available on our companion website (resources.corwin.com/WeeklyWisdom). ●

TRUST YOUR IDEAS

Lisa Dix
17 years

We all know a handful of teachers who get stuck and stale. . . . It is September, so I will pull my September file out and teach what they have always taught every September, no matter the group in front of me or any outside environmental factors. I was hired to teach Grade 4 with a team of two other teachers who had been together for quite some time. They had a "system" of how they did things and did not deviate from "the way things had always been done." My philosophy was more about shaking things up, keeping things interesting, fresh, and fun, so I went against their system throughout the year by doing things MY way—like inviting parents to view a wax museum, sharing pickles on toothpicks and punch because that was a character's idea of fancy in a required novel, assigning monthly reading challenges to increase or instill a love of reading, and hatching chicken eggs complete with birth announcements and pink and blue streamers in the hallway. These fun events and assignments kept my classroom buzzing with engagement. My colleagues constantly were going to the principal to speak to her about me and how, in their opinion, I was not following the curriculum. I am proud of myself for doing what I knew was right, what felt best for the students I was working with.

Since that experience, I have run into the families of that class who have thanked me for helping their children become pleasure readers or who remember the chickens hatching or who still have the poster or project they made from a reading challenge they participated in. I get random comments on Facebook from former students sharing the positive impact I made on their life. THAT is why I went into teaching! It can and does get uncomfortable when you have to deal with negativity and pushback, but my message to new teachers is to do what feels right, march to the beat of your own drum, and knock it out of the park, because it is totally worth it!

These fun events and assignments kept my classroom buzzing with engagement.

Practical Wisdom for the Classroom

I have always believed in the power of humor and have made it a point to laugh with my students, laugh at myself, and share those funny school moments with my family around the dinner table. I wish, in hindsight, I had written a journal full of all the funny comments and happenings to share with new teachers because one thing I know to be true is that we cannot take ourselves too seriously. Laughter is the BEST medicine.

Take Care of You

A year ago, I became a grandmother to a beautiful baby girl who has blessed and changed my life. I am more present in the moments we are together, and I've reevaluated my priorities to put myself and my family first. A FaceTime call, a text image, or a quick weekend visit with my grandchild are enough to restore my soul, settle my brain, put a smile on my face, and reset my attitude so that I am a better person at home and at the office.

••• I LAUGH WITH MY STUDENTS.

PAUSE. REFLECT. ACT.

There will be times when you have to step outside your comfort zone and do what you think is right.

- How does Lisa's message guide you to make decisions that are good for you and your students?
- Are you including your sense of humor in your teaching?
- What will you do this week to support your growth as a teacher?

Write your responses to the prompts in a journal to further your reflection and to help you remember what you are learning. An online journal for your use is available on our companion website (resources.corwin.com/WeeklyWisdom). ●

WEEK

6

BE A TEAM PLAYER

Jennifer Barrientos
9 years

While I worked in a self-contained classroom for children with emotional and behavioral disorders (Grade 2–4) for a teacher who had resigned, I inherited a caseload of six students who had extremely high needs and paraprofessionals who would come and go. My students did not know how to be students; they were merely showing up each day. I was lucky enough to have a behavior specialist who had good relationships with some of the students and responded quickly to big behaviors. There were several instances where the behavior specialist and I had to work in harmony to ensure students were safe and accounted for.

In addition to specific personal experiences, my mentor and supervisor once said to me, "If I'm not part of the problem, I can't be part of the solution." This has been a tenet in my leadership philosophy for years. She means that if I don't figure out what my part in this problem is, it will be very hard for me to find a solution.

I realized that my structures, procedures, and calm presence were the most important aspects of getting through each day. It wasn't my instructional strategies, my knowledge of brand-new techniques, or how Instagram-worthy my classroom was. It was the basics, similar to parenting, that got us through each day. That, and strong communication between the adults.

We had serious behaviors every day for the first few weeks, but because we worked so strongly as a team, our students eventually came around!

I know that when all staff in a classroom are on the same page and demonstrate a unified front, students follow classroom procedures.

I learned that we, as the adults in the classroom, needed to be calm—always. We quickly learned that when we were dysregulated, so were our kids; when we were upset, our kids felt that and reciprocated. We also quickly learned that our little people were going to do what they needed to in order to get what they wanted—which normally meant they would strategically ask the adult that they thought would give it to them! My behavior specialist and I communicated all the time, via text, in person, and via email, before school started, during the day, and after school to debrief. While we communicated constantly, we laughed always.

I know that when all staff in a classroom are on the same page, students follow classroom procedures.

Practical Wisdom for the Classroom

Take the first few weeks of school and practice procedures constantly. You cannot get to academic growth without your students knowing your expectations. Teach every single routine you expect them to do. Revisit your procedures after long weekends, breaks, or whenever you feel you are losing structure.

Take Care of You

I tend to be in "work mode" all the time, and this makes me feel anxious. When I leave my work computer at work and come home to cook dinner, it shifts my focus. When I change my clothes and talk to my son about his day, it helps me to be present in my home life. I also love to read for fun before bed, so I'm not on my phone checking emails. This helps me go to sleep more quickly and to sleep better through the night.

●●● I AM CALM.

PAUSE. REFLECT. ACT.

As you read Jennifer's wisdom this week, assess your level of calm with students in your classroom.

- Do you work in a team and need to align your procedures?
- How are you intentionally shifting from work to home life?
- What will you do this week to support your growth as a teacher?

Write your responses to the prompts in a journal to further your reflection and to help you remember what you are learning. An online journal for your use is available on our companion website (resources.corwin.com/WeeklyWisdom). ●

EMBRACE YOUR MISTAKES

John Radosta
31 years

When I was a very new teacher and terrified that I had neither the knowledge nor the control a teacher should have, I explained a word to the class incorrectly. A student who had always been very active in discussion corrected me, and even though I knew she was right, I was too scared to admit having made a mistake. I thought it would take away from the little credibility I'd earned. Instead, I argued with her until she gave in and agreed I was right. I saw the light go out in her eyes.

Almost immediately, I realized the damage I had done. The student never spoke in class again. I realized that I had prioritized my own comfort over her education—the very thing that was most important—and I had lost the very respect that I thought I was protecting. To this day it is the teaching moment I regret the most.

As painful as the experience was, it was one of the most important lessons I've ever learned—that my first concern in teaching has to be the students' well-being. I also realized that I gain respect by giving it and by admitting I'm a learner too, that I'm not by any means an omniscient expert. In fact, I make multiple mistakes a day, right there in front of the class.

Now, instead of hiding mistakes, I encourage students to correct me in class, and praise their attention and knowledge. I also administer surveys several times a year to measure whether I am reaching them in the best manner possible. I tell them it's my report card, and that since I judge and grade their performance all the time, it's only fair that they get to do the same for me. And then I share the results, good and bad, which holds me publicly accountable. Now I strive to earn their trust, not their respect, and I do it by making myself vulnerable, not by putting on armor. I've found that it helps all of us to learn to take risks—we learn more and in more comfort.

Now, instead of hiding my mistakes,
I encourage students to correct me in class.

Practical Wisdom for the Classroom

For me, time management is stress management. I've had to learn that teaching is a draining job, even as we are givers by nature. I learned that putting every waking moment toward preparing actually made me less prepared because I was too anxious to work adequately with students. By forcing myself to step back and do other things—to have a life away from school—I was happier, more approachable, and better organized.

Take Care of You

It sounds counterintuitive for someone trying to make a good impression as a team player, but I think it's important to be able to say *no* once in a while. There are many opportunities to pitch in at school. But you have to pick the ones that most fulfill your vision of being a good teacher, and the ones that you can best contribute to. Then you can recharge by stepping back and letting others help with the load as well.

●●● I GIVE MYSELF PERMISSION TO SAY *NO*.

PAUSE. REFLECT. ACT.

As you read John's wisdom this week, think about the times you have felt vulnerable.

- How have you managed these emotions?
- Is there something you need to say *no* to?
- What will you do this week to support your growth as a teacher?

Write your responses to the prompts in a journal to further your reflection and to help you remember what you are learning. An online journal for your use is available on our companion website (resources.corwin.com/WeeklyWisdom). ●

8

FIND A MENTOR

Kathi Rogers
50 years

Mentoring new teachers did not exist when I began teaching. You did your student teaching and then when you got a job, you were deemed to be *ready* to go. The department head who hired me over the summer had died, and I came in cold to a department that was struggling to recover. The interim department head was faced with numerous challenges. In my first year, I made tons of mistakes—big and little—thinking I could leave the building for lunch, trying to break up a fight in detention and having my skirt ripped off, allowing a hockey player to nap in my English class while being observed (after having sent him to the office several times for doing just that and getting nowhere). It became clear that the school and I were not a good fit, and I left after one year and went to a neighboring district. At this new district, I was informally mentored by two wonderful colleagues, and I stayed there for the remainder of my career. What made the difference for me was mentoring and the relationships that I made because of it.

What I learned through this experience is that relationships matter in teaching, and mentoring is one of the most important ones for a new teacher. My two mentors listened to me without judgment, took me "off the roof" on bad days, and supported and praised me when I got it right.

What I also learned, and have passed on to new colleagues, is this: when teachers are supported in their first years of teaching, they become better teachers for their students and better colleagues for each other.

What I learned through this experience is that relationships matter in teaching, and mentoring is one of the most important ones for a new teacher.

Practical Wisdom for the Classroom

We were required to give homework assignments each term, and they counted as a specific part of the grade. I wanted homework to be a rein-forcement of things that I had taught in class. Also, as a single parent whose son spent part of his time at his dad's home, I understood that getting homework done was not always given the same priority in differ-ent homes. What I did was give out half a term's worth of homework (in a packet format) at a time with a due date at midterm. Some students would stay with me after school a few days each term to get the work done on time; others would turn it in within a week or so. Some might wait until the last minute. But it gave my students a chance to get reinforce-ment and credit, and parents were grateful for the packets. I always had extra packets for those students who might have left their work at the other parent's home.

Take Care of You

This idea saved me a lot of time in the morning. Plan what you are going to wear to school each day of the week on Sunday night, and put your clothes out for the next day—everything, including jewelry, shoes, and so on. This is one less thing that you have to think about in the morning when—trust me—you will be tired and rushed. Some days the only thing that might go well is how you look! And that is important. I actually kept a "clothing calendar" of what I wore each day. It also helped me to discover what was in my closet and get my money's worth out of my wardrobe. I know it sounds silly, but it worked for me for over thirty years.

••• I DRESS FOR SUCCESS.

PAUSE. REFLECT. ACT.

Kathi's message about finding a mentor is an important one.

- Is there someone at your school who is supporting you?
- How does your professional dress influence your confidence as a teacher?
- What will you do this week to support your growth as a teacher?

Write your responses to the prompts in a journal to further your reflection and to help you remember what you are learning. An online journal for your use is available on our companion website (resources.corwin.com/WeeklyWisdom). ●

GAINING MOMENTUM
FIND YOUR STRENGTHS

As you get your systems established and your students begin to understand the expectations for a classroom community, you need to continue to work from your strengths. Keep reminding yourself of what you love about teaching and why you chose this profession. It may be difficult to remember this on some challenging days! These eight weeks really create a foundation for learning. You are still learning and growing. You will have to continuously implement the routines you introduced at the beginning of the year. Of course, if something doesn't work, this is the time to modify or change it.

The experienced teachers in this season will share their stories, their mistakes, what they learned, and how they integrate positivity, student talents, and ordinary life experiences into their teaching.

Schedule time each week to read and reflect on what is most useful to you, and write your insights in a personal journal or use the online option on the companion website. (Visit the companion website at **resources.corwin .com/WeeklyWisdom.**)

SHARE YOUR LOVE
OF CONTENT

Brooke Traverso
22 years

I have learned a lot in my twenty-two years of teaching, but early on I realized that so many students come into school strongly disliking math. It may be because their parents had a bad experience and shine a negative light on the subject, or the way we teach it, or it may be because they have struggled in math during their previous years in school. Whatever the reason, this breaks my heart as a math lover, and my goal every year is to make my students LOVE math.

I begin each school year telling my students that even if they do not love math today, they will at least like math by Thanksgiving—and they will love math by the end of the school year. They don't believe me, and it becomes a challenge. Throughout the year, we play a lot of math games, both hands-on and online, as well as watch videos and complete the traditional worksheets and whiteboard practice. During every math lesson, I show my students my love for math with enthusiasm and excitement about what we are learning, and we have many discussions about having a growth mindset. Every once in a while, I will ask my students if they have found their love of math yet, and each time I will get more and more students excitedly saying yes.

There is one student in particular who comes to my mind at the start of each school year. It was my first year teaching fourth-grade math and science (thirteen years ago), and she came into my classroom hysterically crying on the second week of school. I pulled her into the hallway, and she expressed to me how much she hated math; she said she could not do it and would never like it. We had a long talk, and I finally calmed her down by telling her that I loved math enough for the both of us, that it was okay she didn't like math YET, and that by the end of our year together, she would LOVE math. She did not believe me, but I think we built enough of a relationship in that conversation that she calmed down and entered the classroom willing to try. Math was very hard for her, and she had many meltdowns that we worked through together; however, it was Thanksgiving week when she pulled me into the hallway with tears in her eyes and asked if she could hug me. I hugged her and asked her what was wrong; her response: "Nothing. I just love math so much now and that is because of you!" Of course, I then started to cry, and we had a nice conversation. The rest of the year was smooth for her; she persevered through hard problems, reached out to me when she needed help, and tried her absolute best. It didn't matter to me how much help she needed or what grades she was getting; what mattered to me was that she LOVED math!

My advice to novice teachers is to exude enthusiasm in all that you do. Your love for learning will shine through your students.

It didn't matter to me how much help she needed or what grades she was getting; what mattered to me was that she LOVED math!

Practical Wisdom for the Classroom

A simple tip that I learned from another teacher and adjusted to work in my classroom is to "freeze" students when giving directions and use a code word prior to transitioning. For example, when I want my students to go from the carpet to their seat, take out their math book, and turn to page 52, I say, "Freeze," and then give all of my directions prior to saying the code word (any fun word or phrase of your choice). Once students hear the code word, they are allowed to go follow the directions. This has helped create smooth transitions in my classroom.

Take Care of You

One way I take care of my body, mind, and spirit is by trying really hard to focus on my family when I am home. It is extremely hard at times, and it especially was in the beginning, but if I look back and could tell myself one thing, it would be to take the time I needed for me. This is something I am still working on, and there are many times that I have to take work home, come in extra early, or stay really late. However, I am trying to go into work early each day and stay for a bit after my students leave to make sure I am ready for the day or days ahead. For me, my children are my world and my happy place. When I am with them, I am at my happiest, so this helps me take care of me!

●●● I AM FULLY PRESENT WITH MY FAMILY.

PAUSE. REFLECT. ACT.

Brooke's story gives us another perspective on our role as teachers.

- How is your love of your content area demonstrated in your classroom?

- How might you adapt her "freeze" routine to work in your classroom?

- What will you do this week to support your growth as a teacher?

Write your responses to the prompts in a journal to further your reflection and to help you remember what you are learning. An online journal for your use is available on our companion website (resources.corwin.com/WeeklyWisdom). ●

10 INTRODUCE YOURSELF AND SAY SOMETHING POSITIVE

Sam Rhode
10 years

When I first started teaching, I had been given the advice to try to contact every parent or guardian of my students, introduce myself, and just talk about something positive that their kids had done in my class. I made it my goal (and still do every year) to do that.

One of my students was considered the tough kid in school. The day after I called his parents, he came into class before school and said that it was the first time that his parents had received good news about him since elementary school, and he thanked me for doing that. I never had any issues with that student in that class all year, and he was always finding ways to be helpful in the classroom.

I think, for me, it is important to allow all students to feel like they are doing the right thing and it is appreciated, and to not create any initial judgment of a student based on past behaviors. They will usually surprise you if you allow them to see that you believe in them and treat them fairly.

. . . it was the first time his parents had received good news about him since elementary school, and he thanked me for doing that.

Practical Wisdom for the Classroom

I had two pieces of advice given to me when I first started, and they were (1) Don't smile until after the holidays and (2) Maintain expectations early on because it is easier to relax later in the year than to have to deal with a rowdy unstructured class the entire year.

Of these, I only follow one. I smile often with my students, and I laugh with them as well. We talk about stuff that is happening outside of the classroom that is important to them, and I try to be empathetic with what they are dealing with. By creating a room of safety and routine, I have found that they are more willing to learn and grow with me. I check in a lot with my students and have discussions with them on behavior and what we can do next time to help the situation. I will usually ask them if there is something that I can do to help them in the future. I care a lot about my students and want them to succeed, and I feel like they understand this, and it helps create a more cohesive classroom.

Take Care of You

For me, I carve out time to go running five to six days a week. I go for about thirty minutes and find that this gives me an opportunity to let things go for that time. I typically don't listen to music when I run, as I find it distracting. I enjoy hearing the wind and listening to my feet hitting the ground and the sound of my breathing. It gives me that time I need to feel like I am taking care of myself. After about ten minutes, I find my mind running through stuff, and that allows me to work through that day and let stuff go.

●●● **I WILL FIND SOMETHING I ENJOY AND DO THAT THIS WEEK.**

PAUSE. REFLECT. ACT.

Sam's story about this student who had not received positive reports for years reminds us of the power of teacher feedback.

- How do you introduce yourself to your parents?

- What is one positive thing you can say about each student in your classroom?

- What will you do this week to support your growth as a teacher?

Write your responses to the prompts in a journal to further your reflection and to help you remember what you are learning. An online journal for your use is available on our companion website (resources.corwin.com/WeeklyWisdom). ●

MAKE A HUMAN CONNECTION WITH EACH STUDENT

Meghan Raftery
18 years

I still feel shame when I remember the words I spoke to my principal two weeks into the school year: "I'm just not sure I can like this child." She paused, turned her whole body toward me and said, "It is your job to find a way."

I never thought I'd have to dig deep to like a *child*, but it turns out my bias, worldview, and humanness prevented me from liking all children by default. Sometimes it takes work to find a connection with a child, but it *is* our job to find it. I returned to my classroom determined to learn more, to empathize with the student and her life story as well as her current strengths and gifts. I discovered a student eager to please when showered with positive reinforcement, a student with a strong sense of independence that could be harnessed toward shared goals when I took the time to talk to her, to know her a little better.

Through this experience, I began to see each of my students as *people* rather than names on a seating chart. It allowed me to share humanity with my students, even the very young ones, and find a way to like every child in my charge.

Sometimes it takes work to find a connection with a child, but it *is* our job to find it.

Practical Wisdom for the Classroom

NEVER engage in a public confrontation with a student. You will not win. Better to defuse the situation (even if it seems like you are ignoring it) and have a private chat with that student. Try to work out a plan of action together that you both can live with. If you need to create a written document that you both sign, do that and review it together at an agreed-upon time.

Take Care of You

Start building your own community. Find educators you admire, enjoy being around, and can learn from—and hold them close! This group will sustain you throughout your career!

●●● I CONNECT WITH EDUCATORS I ENJOY BEING AROUND.

PAUSE. REFLECT. ACT.

Meghan shared her honest feelings in her story of struggling to like a child in her class.

- Has this ever happened to you?

- How did her principal's response influence her next steps?

- What will you do this week to support your growth as a teacher?

Write your responses to the prompts in a journal to further your reflection and to help you remember what you are learning. An online journal for your use is available on our companion website (resources.corwin.com/WeeklyWisdom). ●

DISCOVER YOUR STUDENTS' HIDDEN TALENTS

Mia Pumo
27 years

Relationships matter! It is important for students to feel seen and heard as individuals. All students have gifts and talents even if those are not academic gifts. It is our job as teachers to dig and find those, sometimes hidden, talents and help students to capitalize on them for success. When students feel valued and respected as people, yes, even little people, they will work harder for us. Interview your students to see what they like and what they do after school. Sometimes these talents fit in with the academics, and you may see that keeps them more involved in their academic work.

I learned more about my students when I did home visits. In some cases, my eyes were opened to the bigger picture of what my students were dealing with at home. I saw that many students did not have a lot of support for academic growth, and many had other responsibilities at home. By discovering their own unique gifts, I could focus on that instead of the areas in which they might be struggling.

I learned that every student brings experiences and worries into the classroom, and those cannot be ignored. I learned to take time to let students tell their stories and share what they were interested in with me and their classmates. I knew when to let a student take some quiet time or when a student needed to share. This is how I helped them learn.

I learned that when students feel valued and respected as people, they will work harder for us.

Practical Wisdom for the Classroom

Students need to understand the *why*, so have conversations up front about classroom expectations and why they exist. I made it clear, so my students understood what I expected in their behavior. I kept detailed records of every interaction with a student who was struggling, so I had a record of my conversations to share with parents and administrators. Even though there are difficult challenges with some students, I still believe in offering genuine praise often. I find this is the best way to build relationships.

Take Care of You

Take advantage of holiday breaks to refresh and recharge. Don't use it as time to catch up on bundles of papers that you didn't get to. Also, I developed a morning routine, which was life changing. I started getting up half an hour earlier to journal, stretch, meditate, and pray over my day. It was a game changer. You can't pour from an empty cup.

●●● I SHARE THE *WHY* WITH MY STUDENTS.

PAUSE. REFLECT. ACT.

One way to build relationships with our students is to highlight their strengths.

- How will you intentionally discover your students' hidden talents?

- Is there a way to integrate your students' gifts into the academic subject you teach?

- What will you do this week to support your growth as a teacher?

Write your responses to the prompts in a journal to further your reflection and to help you remember what you are learning. An online journal for your use is available on our companion website (resources.corwin.com/WeeklyWisdom). ●

REFLECTIONS

WEEK
13

ACCEPT ADVICE GRACEFULLY

Diane Mackie
39 years

In my first year of teaching, I was working with the English supervisor who told me my teaching was too one sided. She wanted me to know that I was lecturing too much and not involving the students in their own learning. At first, I didn't know what to say because all I knew was to stand up in front of the room and talk. Her mentoring helped me to find more ways to directly involve the students in their own learning instead of them passively hearing my voice. I learned that if students are not actively involved in their own learning, then they do not absorb as much information and don't succeed in school.

She helped me to understand and learn a variety of teaching and learning methods to use to change this. I am so glad I was able to hear her suggestions because it is not always easy to hear you are doing something ineffective. Her style and willingness to help me grow made the difference and helped me begin my career successfully.

I was lecturing too much
and not involving the students
in their own learning.

Practical Wisdom for the Classroom

I would start out my class in the same way each day by centering the students and getting them focused on the English classroom. Centering means to enter quietly and start the activity that is on the board as they enter. There were routines in place for large-group and small-group work. All the students knew what they were supposed to be doing when they entered the room. This allowed me time to also transition, and then I could begin the class formally when I was ready.

Take Care of You

Find a physical activity that helps you center, for example, swimming, walking, running, yoga—and do it regularly, if not every day. It helps to clear your mind and focus on you for a bit. By moving my body, I relax my mind. This helps to create balance and relieve stress.

PAUSE. REFLECT. ACT.

In Diane's story, you can see how she was open to her supervisor's suggestions, and because of this, she improved her teaching quickly.

- How much time do you spend talking in your classroom?

- How much time do your students spend talking or engaged in activities?

- What will you do this week to support your growth as a teacher?

Write your responses to the prompts in a journal to further your reflection and to help you remember what you are learning. An online journal for your use is available on our companion website (resources.corwin.com/WeeklyWisdom). ●

BE COMPASSIONATE

Mary-Margaret Mara
30 years

I had one student in my second year of teaching named Richard (not his real name) who challenged me on a daily basis through his behavior and inappropriate actions toward others in the classroom. I remember thinking that if he just wasn't one of my students, I would have a great class. He is also the one student who forever changed the way that I teach by changing my perspective on my students and on myself.

My attitude toward Richard changed the day I did a home visit to the small one-bedroom apartment where he lived with his mother, brother, and sister. A drive-by shooting had shot a bullet into their apartment, and this was the catalyst for the visit. Seeing the world he lived in changed how I saw him, brought me to tears, and helped me realize that this little boy was just trying to survive with the weight of the world on his shoulders.

The experience with Richard shifted my perspective of him and made me rethink who I wanted to be as an educator. Our students have stories, and their behavior is a form of communication. I learned from Richard that treating every child with kindness and compassion will help build relationships and open the doors for learning.

Our students have stories, and their behavior is a form of communication.

Practical Wisdom for the Classroom

I offer a weekly Kindness award to one student who shows kindness and respect to peers, teachers, and family. I invite students to nominate students they see being kind, and this keeps everyone "looking" for kind actions all week. This student receives a personalized certificate and an extra prize for the week. My goal is for every student to receive an award at some point during the year.

Take Care of You

I live to walk and listen to mindfulness podcasts. I feel like it helps me reach a place of calm, reset my mind, and gain perspective on what is important to me. It is important for me to take care of myself so that I have the energy to then take care of my students.

••• I RESET MY MIND WHEN I WALK.

PAUSE. REFLECT. ACT.

As you read Mary-Margaret's wisdom this week, think about what stands out to you about her change in attitude.

- How do you get your students to "see" kind actions in your classroom?

- Have you ever listened to a mindfulness podcast? What did you learn from that experience?

- What will you do this week to support your growth as a teacher?

Write your responses to the prompts in a journal to further your reflection and to help you remember what you are learning. An online journal for your use is available on our companion website (resources.corwin.com/WeeklyWisdom). ●

15

REMEMBER IT TAKES A VILLAGE

Alicia Desrochers
6 years

The biggest thing I've learned as a teacher is that the saying "It takes a village to raise a child" is absolutely true. Every single child in your class has a village, and you are only part of that child's village. To best serve a student, you should make sure you are working with that village. That means making connections with students' families and guardians, athletic coaches, their favorite teachers from last year, and other significant people in their lives. It's amazing how big a difference it can make when students see that you are a part of the village and engaged with each student's whole support network.

Students respect when teachers recognize that they are people with opinions. When things aren't working well, I know I can always talk to my students and brainstorm solutions together. We have had meetings about cell phone policies in class, late work policies, and how we should conduct ourselves during group work, and all of these conversations have made a better classroom for both students and teachers.

Students sometimes have better solutions to problems than we give them credit for. But more importantly, students are the most important part of our classroom and community, and they deserve to have their voices heard.

There are many things in your classroom that don't have to be just "because I said so." Consider collaborating with your students whenever possible and inviting them into the process; their buy-in is well worth the time to have the discussion.

When things aren't working well, I know I can always talk to my students and brainstorm solutions together.

Practical Wisdom for the Classroom

Students love being recognized for the positive things they do. If you have a difficult student, catch that student doing something good as early in the year as possible, even if it's a small thing. Then, call, text, or email home to give a "shout out" for that thing. This both helps develop a good relationship with the guardian, but also shows the student that you recognize the good too.

The old saying is "Students don't learn for teachers they don't like," and I believe that's true; making these positive connections builds the relationships, which helps them want to learn for you.

Take Care of You

I like to take a long walk after work. I've done different types of exercise too, and they all help, but there's something about being outside, getting fresh air, listening to an audiobook or music, and not thinking about work for an hour or so that feels really good. It helps me relax and re-center myself, separating work time from home time, so I can relax when I get home and leave work for the next day.

●●● I SEE THE POSITIVE IN ALL OF MY STUDENTS.

PAUSE. REFLECT. ACT.

Alicia presents an idea that includes the students and other members of the school community as part of the "village" that is supporting all students.

- How does this idea relate to you and your image of your classroom?

- How will you use Alicia's suggestions for management and self-care?

- What will you do this week to support your growth as a teacher?

Write your responses to the prompts in a journal to further your reflection and to help you remember what you are learning. An online journal for your use is available on our companion website (resources.corwin.com/WeeklyWisdom). ●

WHEN YOU FALL DOWN, GET BACK UP!

Melissa Carr
32 years

In my early years of teaching, I did not have a remote control to turn on the classroom television. Teachers were last to get such modern technology! Instead, I had to climb on a chair to manually turn on the TV, which was bolted to the wall. One day, I took a wrong step and fell off the chair to the floor behind my desk. My class of ninth graders fell silent.

Thinking quickly, I jumped up from behind desk and said, "When you fall, it's always important to get back up!"

The class erupted into laughter and clapped. After that, they always enjoyed hearing my life's foibles and laughing with me. I learned to integrate humor into my teaching as much as possible so as to engage my students and keep a lighthearted connection with them.

Not taking myself so seriously and laughing at myself when I made a mistake—or literally stumbled—helped me to be the kind of teacher that connects with my students. It helped my students understand that mistakes are not catastrophes if you can get up and keep going. It let my students see me as a human being—just like them.

Making connections with students quickly is the best investment in creating a classroom culture of trust and safety. When I shared my stories, I not only modeled how to start a piece of writing with what you know but also created rapport and trust with my students, who learned to take academic risks for the rest of our time together. Once students feel connected to you and their classmates, and know that mistakes are part of learning, you can set higher expectations that they strive to meet because of the foundational relationship.

When you fall down, get back up.

Practical Wisdom

Not everything needs a grade! Get students to agree on which pieces of writing should be graded and allow them to provide verbal feedback to one another. You can also teach students how to grade each other and give them criteria. You will have some assistants and future teachers in your class if you teach them how to grade papers. They will also become better writers themselves as they learn to identify the strengths and weaknesses in the work of others.

Take Care of You

Use one weekend day to disconnect completely. No planning or grading to be done. Focus on you and not the job.

••• I SCHEDULE TIME TO DISCONNECT FROM SCHOOLWORK ON THE WEEKEND.

PAUSE. REFLECT. ACT.

Melissa's story of falling down and being able to laugh about it showed her ability to be in the moment and add some humor to the situation.

- How do you integrate your sense of humor and laughter into your classroom?
- Why is it important to teach our students how to assess their own work?
- What will you do this week to support your growth as a teacher?

Write your responses to the prompts in a journal to further your reflection and to help you remember what you are learning. An online journal for your use is available on our companion website (resources.corwin.com/WeeklyWisdom). ●

STAYING IN THE FLOW
FOCUS ON TEACHING AND LEARNING
WEEKS 17–30

Now you are in the flow. Your students know what the expectations are for their participation and good behavior, and you have the systems in place. It doesn't mean you won't have any challenges or bad days—in fact you will. It just means you are better equipped to respond to the unpredictable life of a teacher in a more graceful way. These fourteen weeks are prime teaching and learning time. This is when you and your students will show the most growth if you focus and stay on track. Now more than ever, you need to revisit your management strategies for routines and behavior. TIME is always going to be an issue, so face it head on and don't allow yourself to get swamped in paperwork. This is the time for personal attention to YOU, so you don't overdo and stress.

The experienced teachers contributing to this chapter will share their stories—their mistakes, what they learned, and how they embraced their own style of teaching, used student voices to check in on their own progress, and continued to show up at school (even when they didn't want to!).

Schedule time each week to read and reflect on what is most useful to you, and write your insights in a personal journal or use the online option on the companion website. (Visit the companion website at **resources.corwin .com/WeeklyWisdom.**)

GIVE STUDENTS THE TOOLS TO SHINE

Sandra J. Brower
15 years

I had one young student, in ninth grade at the time, who would come into my classroom regularly and complain about one of her teachers. The teacher was too strict, too mean. My young friend would rattle off all of the things the teacher did or said that were stupid or mean. Knowing the teacher as a colleague and friend, I knew that she did have certain expectations, yet she cared very much about the well-being of her students. So, one day, when this student came in, upset again by what her teacher had said or done, I challenged her to ask the teacher questions about some of her favorite things to do, what she liked, and to begin looking for three things about the teacher that she did like. A few days later, my student came in all smiles and began to tell me some "really cool" things about her teacher.

The interesting piece to the story is this young girl tended to be what we would call a troubled child. She would often be late to class, skip classes, or on occasion harass or intimidate other students, and she struggled to pass her courses. Students like this are often struggling with so much and need someone to teach them the skills, give them the tools they need, and guide them to do good and seek out the good.

This encounter and connection completely changed my life's course and career. My master's degree is in health education, my bachelor's in psychology. I went on to pursue several certifications in the field of positive psychology, the science of human flourishing and well-being. Bringing this science into the classroom, into schools and school communities, is a major focus and passion of mine. My learning included seeing these "troubled" students differently. They may seem tough and closed off, but they are still children and desire to have an adult see them, hear them, and guide them.

My experience taught me first to see the student as a learner on life's journey and then to ask myself, What does this child need? As educators, we are here to teach them math, reading, science, and history, but we also have the greatest of opportunities to teach them practices that inform their well-being. Human beings desire to be happy and live a life of meaning and purpose.

We are wired to seek the good, the things in life that make us happy. Our brains like to be happy; it releases dopamine and makes us feel good. If our environment primarily provides us with opportunities to practice gratitude, positive social connections, and kindness, we will develop "healthy habits" in order to be happy. These and other skills are all important to living our best lives. Becoming a positive educator can help us all do that.

My experience has taught me first to see the student as a learner on life's journey and then to ask myself, What does this child need?

Practical Wisdom for the Classroom

Those times we just react, not giving ourselves the time and space to think, that is when our emotional brain is in charge. This reaction shuts down our rational thinking brain. I teach my students about the triune brain theory: the emotional brain, rational brain, and lizard brain and what each controls, giving examples and asking them to come up with some of their own. I then share something my mother always said, but I never understood until I started learning about positive psychology: "Count to ten before you scream."

As you are counting to ten, you breathe, you give yourself the space you need to calm the emotional brain and to allow the rational brain to engage. I teach the kids to respect the space, breathe, count to ten, breathe. And I do it too.

Take Care of You

Taking care of our body, mind, and spirit requires us to practice multiple ways to care for our whole self, but if I were to choose one, it would be nature. Any time in nature fills my senses and nourishes my mind, body, and soul.

●●● **I EXPERIENCE NATURE WITH ALL OF MY SENSES.**

PAUSE. REFLECT. ACT.

Sandra's connection with this young girl completely changed her life's course and the direction of her career.

- How are your students influencing you?

- How are you integrating a focus on your students' well-being into your classroom curriculum?

- What will you do this week to support your growth as a teacher?

Write your responses to the prompts in a journal to further your reflection and to help you remember what you are learning. An online journal for your use is available on our companion website (resources.corwin.com/WeeklyWisdom). ●

GET HELP WHEN YOU NEED IT

Traci Rizzo
25 years

In my first year of teaching, I was hired to teach a first-second grade combination class across the country in southern California. These students did not yet know how to read, and I realized I did not feel that I knew enough about the science of reading from my undergraduate program to teach them. I knew how to follow a manual, but I did not know how to teach children to read!

I sought out and formed a relationship with the reading specialist at the school and began to learn how to teach children to read, which would later inspire me to continue my education to earn my master's of reading. Thanks to her guidance (teaching me, giving me professional books to read, inspiring me), I discovered my passion within teaching.

To this day, twenty-five years later, I believe that it's very important to connect with colleagues. These connections are your lifeline, your continued education. Don't be intimidated—there are no silly questions.

These connections are your lifeline, your continued education.

Practical Wisdom for the Classroom

Schedule yourself! Set daily time aside to catch up on the work you haven't finished. And when that time is up, put it away. And on the days that you just need a complete break, take the break. The to-do list never ends, but the day does. Yes, there will be days when you do double time and feel great after the work is done, and that's great. Just don't make that the norm.

Take Care of You

Yoga and connecting with family and friends work for me. It may take time to figure out what works for you, but you don't know unless you try. Goat yoga anyone?

••• I STOP WHEN MY SCHEDULED TIME TO WORK IS OVER.

PAUSE. REFLECT. ACT.

Traci's story about not knowing how to teach something happens to all of us at some point. The key is to reach out and get some help when you need it.

- What area of your teaching is lacking?

- Who could help you?

- What will you do this week to support your growth as a teacher?

Write your responses to the prompts in a journal to further your reflection and to help you remember what you are learning. An online journal for your use is available on our companion website (resources.corwin.com/WeeklyWisdom). ●

19

USE RELEVANCE TO ENGAGE STUDENTS

Serena Pariser
16 years

It's important to remember that deep down, all students want to learn. Some students will do whatever a teacher asks them to do. However, some students, for motivation to come, must see the relevance and purpose in what they are doing and learning. We'll always have both types of learners in our classroom. It's essential that, as teachers, we connect our lessons to the real world.

I remember the first time I tried a true problem-based learning unit from start to finish. In a nutshell, students were asked to choose a societal issue in groups, research it, and make a presentation. They had to research what the world was trying to do to resolve the issue and explain why they thought these solutions weren't working. I then asked them to critically think and create an alternative, elegant solution that hadn't been tried yet, since what the world was trying to do to stop the societal problem wasn't working—or the problem wouldn't still exist. The last part of the unit was to present the solution to an authentic audience.

Wow. Wow. Wow. I was blown away by the engagement, lack of behavior issues (almost nonexistent during this unit), and pure excitement of the students. Also, I noticed that I was energized after classes, rather than exhausted, because the student engagement was so high, and energy was positive in the classroom.

Witnessing this changed my teaching career because I realized that when students see relevance—are given the opportunity to be creative and think critically, work collaboratively, and know their voice is valued by an authentic audience—learning will soar.

> Wow. Wow. Wow. I was blown away by the engagement, lack of behavior issues (almost nonexistent during this unit), and pure excitement of the students.

Practical Wisdom for the Classroom

I always have a class opening routine. It's the same three or four steps, in the same order, every single day. It might look like this: "Welcome Period 2. (1) Take out your homework and place it on the corner of your desk. (2) Write today's homework in your planner. (3) Begin reading your independent reading book."

This means I can take attendance, check in with an individual student or two, perhaps check homework, and do the little things before the lesson without disruption.

I find that playing calming music as they walk in and pointing to the projected slide works to start class off on the right foot. When a student is a little lost as to what to do, all I have to do is point to the slide instead of repeating myself like a broken record, which could potentially disturb the calmness for the rest of the students.

You can use the same slide for the entire day, week, or even longer; just change the class name before a new group of students enters. You won't have to say a word. Just point to the slide. Your life as a teacher is much easier with a consistent beginning-of-class routine.

Take Care of You

Sign up for some activity you enjoy that forces you to unplug for a few hours each week. This should be something that energizes you—whether you go to a gym, a yoga studio, a painting class, a board game club, a book club, a weekly meditation group, or a social sports league. Try your best to keep this commitment every week because you'll be surprised how much more present you'll be in the classroom after this activity. Trust me! There's always going to be one more thing to do; that's the nature of teaching. But the most successful and balanced teachers know how to unplug and do it regularly without guilt.

••• I AM ENERGIZED BY MY STUDENTS' ENGAGEMENT.

PAUSE. REFLECT. ACT.

Serena's story of taking the time to create engaging, relevant activities gives us a plan for energizing our students and ourselves.

- What will you do to make your content relevant?

- How will this motivate those learners who want to know why you are teaching this content?

- What will you do this week to support your growth as a teacher?

Write your responses to the prompts in a journal to further your reflection and to help you remember what you are learning. An online journal for your use is available on our companion website (resources.corwin.com/WeeklyWisdom). ●

GIVE FEEDBACK TO SUPPORT STUDENT GROWTH

Jenna Monahan
19 years

I worked on a team where the math teacher didn't use number or letter grades with his students on any assignments or projects. Instead of giving a B+ with no real comment, he opted to list each standard in the math curriculum and provide feedback on each skill or understanding. I taught English language arts and wasn't totally sure how this type of system would look in my subject area, and since no one else in our building was using this approach, I was too scared, tired, and stressed to try it out on my own.

Then last year, our whole team decided to "take the plunge"; all of us would pilot the use of feedback on assessed skills or understandings. It was terrifying, and we did get a little pushback from parents who wanted to know if their child got an A grade on each assignment. But the majority of parents and the administration were really excited that we were trying an approach that shared specific feedback with each student instead of just a number or letter.

Our goal as a team was for students to be able to say, "This is what I know, and this is what I am working on" rather than just saying, "I have a B+." Another goal was to create a more equitable grading policy and measure of student understanding. Good behavior, neatness, attendance, participation, and effort are all important on a term report, but they do not always correlate to understanding the subject matter.

The biggest sign of success I noticed was how this grading shift impacted two students who had struggled under the traditional grading model. One student had refused to come to school and almost left the previous year; another earned mostly Ds and Fs. Both flourished when given specific feedback on a standard. This new system of sharing feedback and identifying gaps in understanding gave us more insight as to what these students DID know about the subject.

Our team saw both of these students consistently show progress, and both ultimately earned B grades at the end of the term. We presented our findings to the staff at the end of the year, and this year, twenty staff members are collaborating to revamp how they give feedback and grade students.

The biggest sign of success for me was seeing how this grading shift impacted two students who had struggled in the past.

Practical Wisdom for the Classroom

This one took me a long time to really be comfortable with—you don't need to "grade" everything. I tell students that some of what they do is practice, and I will walk around and see what they are doing and use that evidence to reteach or clarify concepts based on what I am seeing. When it is time to give formal feedback, I am able to give better and more prompt feedback if I focus on two or three skills on a rubric, rather than all of them at once. Once you've mastered those two things, you can move on.

Take Care of You

Teaching may be a passion and a huge part of your life and identity, but it IS NOT YOUR LIFE. For me, this ebbs and flows, and especially during the pandemic, the lines between work and home got very fuzzy. But I made it a personal goal to get that balance back. I commit to leaving work at a specific time each day, and no matter what, I leave. If something isn't ready, I prioritize getting in early, so I can get it ready. I do not bring work home no matter what. School is my career; school is not my entire life.

••• I MAINTAIN MY BALANCE WITH HEALTHY CHOICES.

PAUSE. REFLECT. ACT.

The classroom research in Jenna's story illustrated that the new system not only helped students, it inspired more teachers to create better ways to show student progress.

- What's your grading system?

- Is it helping students grow? How?

- What will you do this week to support your growth as a teacher?

Write your responses to the prompts in a journal to further your reflection and to help you remember what you are learning. An online journal for your use is available on our companion website (resources.corwin.com/WeeklyWisdom). ●

21

USE STUDENT SURVEYS TO ASSESS YOUR TEACHING

Tyler Brundage
6 years

My first year teaching music, I had a rough seventh-grade class. Like many new teachers, I was afraid to implement too many rules and restrictions because I worried students would think I was too strict, and I would not be able to build a rapport with them. I used some of the anonymous student surveys that Carol Pelletier Radford had mentioned in her *Mentoring in Action* book to see what the students thought of the class and me. The class unanimously told me they thought that they had a great relationship with me but wished the other students would stop acting out. They told me they wanted more structure and for me to hold them more accountable.

Through this experience, I learned the power of the student voice in building a rapport with my class. We discussed the results of the survey, and many were relieved to see that their peers felt the same way they did. We talked as a group about what our expectations were and what appropriate consequences should be for not meeting those expectations. Once we had this conversation, there was a noticeable, positive shift in the energy of the class. My students were responding well to the new set of expectations, and I was able to solidify a rapport with my students because they saw I genuinely valued their thoughts and opinions.

After this experience, I have made it a point to implement the student voice survey and use it to guide how I run my class and how I implement my lessons. We start every year with an anonymous survey asking what they need from me, their peers, and themselves to be successful. We go over what they think classroom expectations should be and what an appropriate consequence should be for not meeting these expectations. In rehearsals, I talk to the kids about what skill sets they need to work on or what sections of their music need a little extra attention. I tell my students all the time, "This is your program, not mine. Everything we do in this room is for you." And because of that, they feel valued and take ownership of their work, their performances, and their program.

I have made it a point to implement the student voice survey and use it to guide how I run my class and how I implement my lessons.

Practical Wisdom for the Classroom

One time management issue novice teachers face is having students "finish" before the bell rings. This is often when disruption and chaos break out, so it is important to have a few activities that students can do at the end of the class or other times you think the kids need a brain break. Just make sure the students aren't finishing early so they can do that fun activity at the end of the class.

Take Care of You

If you need to work outside of the school day—grading, planning, writing emails, etc.—give yourself an hour or two. Set a timer, and as soon as it goes off, you are done regardless of what is finished. If you know you have only so much time to complete these tasks, it forces you to prioritize what really needs to get done. Adhering to this practice will prevent you from working 24/7, and it significantly reduces the chances of burnout.

●●● **I PRIORITIZE WHAT NEEDS TO BE DONE NEXT.**

PAUSE. REFLECT. ACT.

Tyler's message shows us that by using anonymous surveys throughout the year, we can gather student perspectives and use them to improve our teaching.

- How would you use a student survey in your classroom, and what questions would you include?

- What types of activities will you use to minimize disruption at the end of class?

- What will you do this week to support your growth as a teacher?

Write your responses to the prompts in a journal to further your reflection and to help you remember what you are learning. An online journal for your use is available on our companion website (resources.corwin.com/WeeklyWisdom). ●

BE YOUR AUTHENTIC SELF

Chandra Joseph-Lacet
28 years

One of the most memorable and defining moments of my teaching career was one Friday when I rolled up my carpet and told my principal I wouldn't be back on Monday. I was exhausted, and it was just too hard to do everything. I wasn't keeping up with my counterparts. My principal looked at me and said, "I'll see you on Monday—and remember, I hired Chandra to be a teacher. Make sure you bring her back with you Monday morning."

When my principal said that I had no idea what he was talking about, but it has never left me. I was spending way too much time comparing myself to the teachers around me, trying to plan like Ms. Dimondapolis, trying to make my classroom management match Mr. Russell's, trying to do everything the way the others were doing it with what appeared to be flawless effort. I was twisting myself in knots to teach the way "they" taught. So much so, that I left who I was outside of my classroom door.

There's no growth in trying to be something that you are not. I had to find my own path. I had to be myself and experience my own journey to be able to develop and grow. I had to be me, and I had to stop comparing myself to those around me.

Bringing Chandra with me every day, along with the challenges and successes I experience, has definitely been my greatest teacher. Being myself and bringing my entire self into the classroom allowed me to relax and gave me the confidence to take risks and try on new teaching strategies in my own time and in my own way. Sometimes it worked beautifully, and sometimes it didn't, but either way, I learned something about myself and my teaching. Being my authentic self in my classroom allowed me to admit what I didn't know and needed to learn, while at the same time allowing me to build muscle and strengthen and refine along the way. This was and continues to be a very humbling but rewarding journey. Stand tall and try hard not to compare yourself to those around you. Be you and know that the only teacher you should be comparing yourself to is the teacher you were yesterday or last year.

I had to find my own path. I had to be myself and experience my own journey to be able to develop and grow.

Practical Wisdom for the Classroom

The most important tip I can give any teacher is to invest the time up front to get to know your students and their families and to allow them to get to know you. RELATIONSHIPS ARE EVERYTHING!!! This is how a classroom community is built. Students need to be seen and heard. Students want to know who you are and that you care about them.

There is no number of classroom contracts, shared norms, expectations, or routines that will ever replace building authentic relationships with students and families. This is a game changer. Remember, it's not a U-Haul, it's a We-Haul. And the *we* is you, any other adults who work in the classroom, and all of your students and their families. Take the time to build personalized connections with those around you.

This heart-work is worth the effort. Come from a place of genuine care, mutual respect, and positivity and you will spend much less time on behavioral challenges and consequences and much more time on experiencing the joy of teaching and learning.

Take Care of You

This is something I wish I had learned MUCH earlier in my career. Here it is: no matter how many hours you put in, no matter how long you stay up and plan and grade, there will always be more work to do. There, I said it. That's the honest truth. Understand that and let it sink in. Once you accept it, then you can come to realize there truly are only so many hours in a day, so you must prioritize and CHOOSE how you will spend those hours.

And when I say prioritize, I mean your entire life, not just your teacher life. You are much more than your classroom. You must schedule in YOU every day to make YOU a priority. In the world of teaching, if it isn't on the schedule, it may as well not exist. I've seen far too many teachers, both early-career teachers and veterans, burn out because they didn't schedule time for themselves or prioritize their well-being. Don't think that you'll get to yourself later because you probably won't. Take time: time to pause, time to laugh, time to listen, time to read, time to be still, time to eat, time to rest . . . and SCHEDULE IT IN. Literally. You would be surprised how even a small amount of YOU time every day can provide what you need to recover and reenergize. Don't lose YOU in this profession. YOU are too important. And remember, being a martyr never ends well.

●●● I WILL SCHEDULE TIME FOR MYSELF.

PAUSE. REFLECT. ACT.

This story is about the importance of bringing your authentic self into the classroom every day.

- What do you do well? What are your strengths?

- Where have you grown so far this year? How do you know?

- What will you do this week to support your growth as a teacher?

Write your responses to the prompts in a journal to further your reflection and to help you remember what you are learning. An online journal for your use is available on our companion website (resources.corwin.com/WeeklyWisdom). ●

SEE KINDNESS IN ACTION

Sarah Berger
10 years

The students I taught my fourth year of teaching forever changed the way I teach. They were far from perfect kids, but they worked hard and were constantly encouraging each other to be the best version of themselves. They were the kind of group you never forget. After we returned from our winter holiday break, a new student joined our class. He was new to our state, and this life transition was a truly tough one for him. He had a lot of behaviors I had never dealt with as a teacher, and he did not come with the support needed for these types of behaviors.

Being his teacher for four short months changed my philosophy as a teacher and the way I work with every person I have met moving forward. It was not the behaviors he exhibited or the perseverance I developed from learning to handle these behaviors that changed me. It was watching my fourth-grade students. The amazing group of students I was blessed to teach that year welcomed this student, who completely changed their world at school in a way none of us expected, without missing a beat.

They were kind to him, worked hard to show him kindness, and included him to the best of their ability. On the days I felt pulled too thin to keep going, I saw these precious ten-year-olds come to school each day ready to show kindness no matter what. The biggest thing I took from that short time is that you truly never know what someone is carrying, and meeting people with kindness makes all the difference.

> On the days I felt pulled too thin to keep going, I saw these precious ten-year-olds come to school each day ready to show kindness no matter what.

Practical Wisdom for the Classroom

Time management is still an area I work on. My grandmother worked in education her entire career and taught me three things: (1) to-do lists can be your most powerful tool, (2) you can accomplish a lot in twenty focused minutes, and (3) "eat that frog!" first. Eat that frog is a strategy she taught me from a book about tackling hard tasks. When looking at my list of things needing to get done, I get those important, yet not so enjoyable, tasks done first, so they aren't put off until the last minute. It is much more difficult to get things done that you don't enjoy when you are exhausted; I focus on those first so that I don't get bogged down later.

Take Care of You

My students need me to be the best version of myself, and most of the time, that means leaving my computer at work and tending to myself when I get home. That has meant different things for me in different seasons of my life. It used to be long baths and face masks. Now that I have my own children, it is spending time being a mama and exercising. I try to spend at least a little time each evening doing something that truly brings my soul joy.

●●● I WILL EAT THE FROG FIRST!

PAUSE. REFLECT. ACT.

We often miss the magic in our classroom because we are paying attention to other details that may not be as important.

- How are the students in your classes helping each other and being kind?

- What are the most challenging tasks for you? Do you eat the frog first or put off that difficult, important task for last?

- What will you do this week to support your growth as a teacher?

Write your responses to the prompts in a journal to further your reflection and to help you remember what you are learning. An online journal for your use is available on our companion website (resources.corwin.com/WeeklyWisdom). ●

GET TO THE ROOT CAUSE

Stacey Hervey
24 years

I learned this technique in training I attended that addressed ways to reduce recidivism and juvenile delinquency in schools. One principle that resonated with me, and that I use daily, is finding the root cause of an issue. Students are a puzzle. We must learn how to solve the puzzle to help them be successful. Students also rarely expand on answers unless you ask the right questions. Doing a deep dive into a problem can provide interesting results. I rely on the "Five Whys" concept to find out more about an issue.

For example, a student was five minutes late every single day. When I dug deeper, I discovered that the student was taking the bus, and it took about an hour to get to school every day. He could either get on the bus at 5:30 am or 6:30 am. He chose the 6:30 bus and arrived at 7:40. We developed a plan for him to do an extra "warm up" to account for time missed. We also had a conversation with the other students, so they understood why he was late. Students were fine with his tardiness, knowing that the only other alternative was arriving at school an hour before it started.

Instead of just marking this student tardy every single day, which might lead to the student deciding not to come to school at all, we solved the problem by getting to the root cause.

. . . we solved the problem by getting to the root cause.

Practical Wisdom for the Classroom

I have always worked in urban schools where some students are coming to us from families that cannot create environments conducive to healthy student learning. I struggled with this at the beginning of my career, as students shared some of their life struggles with me. What I learned is not to decrease the rigor for students in an attempt to alleviate what they are going through at home. I needed to make sure my assignments were aligned to standards and not just "easy" to make up for their home situation.

Take Care of You

Make sure you have friends outside of school. Everyone you know should not be a teacher or connected to your work life. Having a hobby helps a lot. If you don't have one, think about what you used to do when you were a kid and pick it up again. I also recommend that you hang out with people who make you laugh a lot!

••• I LAUGH OUT LOUD WITH FRIENDS.

PAUSE. REFLECT. ACT.

Stacey's story encourages us to maintain our standards even when student success seems almost impossible.

- Who are the students in your classroom that need modified lessons to succeed?

- How will you modify lessons and maintain the rigor?

- What will you do this week to support your growth as a teacher?

Write your responses to the prompts in a journal to further your reflection and to help you remember what you are learning. An online journal for your use is available on our companion website (resources.corwin.com/WeeklyWisdom). ●

WEEK

25 CHANGE THE WAY YOU LOOK AT YOUR FAILURES

Maryanne Margiotta
23 years

It bombed! That's all I could think of as I drove home from school. That lesson plan that I had so carefully constructed, planned for, and researched—the one I was so excited to present to my energetic group of ninth-graders, certain they would love it and learn from it and beg their teacher to repeat it. *Yeah, right.* It *bombed*, and that's all I could think of that night—and the next day, and the next.

I realized later that my mood had changed and colored my perspective those next few days of school that year. I felt defeated, and it showed in my energy, my optimism, and my outlook. The tone in my classroom was different because *I* was different. And I didn't like the feeling.

Luckily, I talked about it—to a friend who wasn't a teacher but knew enough about kids, and about *me*, to understand. "You can't change how it went," she told me, "but you can change how you frame it." Simple, yes—but true. I let one experience color my attitude. And my attitude sets the tone for the entire class.

I learned from that experience, and in all the years since, that there are many, many joys in teaching—moments that remind you why you entered this profession. But there will also be many bumps along the way. That lesson *did* bomb, but so have others. And there have been many impossibly chaotic days, juggling school responsibilities along with the many other balls in our lives. But I have learned not to let any bump color my perspective. My students need me to set the tone in our classroom. Plans that "bomb" aren't the end of the world and don't need to change my perspective. Unless I *let* them.

Plans that "bomb" aren't the end of the world and don't need to change my perspective.

Practical Wisdom for the Classroom

Be consistent! Whatever routines you have in place in your class, stick by them! I noticed my classroom management became easier when my students knew what was expected of them and that there was consistency in my approach.

Take Care of You

When you're a beginning teacher, it's HARD not to be thinking of your job at all hours of the day and night! But it's important that you do everything you can to carve out that special time each day for whatever makes you happy. And don't feel guilty about it (those papers to correct CAN WAIT!). Just that time away to do what matters most to you will recharge you!

●●● I WILL TAKE SOME *ME* TIME THIS WEEK.

PAUSE. REFLECT. ACT.

We all have lessons that fail. The important message in Maryanne's story is what we do when the lesson bombs.

- What do you do when your lesson doesn't work out as planned? Is it a healthy reaction?

- What are your favorite *me* time activities, and when do you do them?

- What will you do this week to support your growth as a teacher?

Write your responses to the prompts in a journal to further your reflection and to help you remember what you are learning. An online journal for your use is available on our companion website (resources.corwin.com/WeeklyWisdom). ●

REFLECTIONS

HONOR YOUR
TEACHING STYLE

Erin Jacobson
16 years

At the beginning of my career, I wanted to be successful, and I watched the teachers around me to see what they were doing. I didn't always feel confident in my style as it was quiet, and I used a softer voice than some of the other teachers.

My classroom was right next to the school counselor's office. One day she caught me while my students were at the gym and said, "I love listening to you teach. The way you speak to the kids is so kind and clear." Her comment really touched me. I learned through this interaction that I could keep being me. I didn't need to be tougher or sterner. I didn't need to copy anyone else's teaching style or how they talked with their students. My style was accepted and acknowledged by another person who saw me in action at the school. It felt so good to know that being me was okay! This one small comment from this counselor encouraged me to keep doing what I was doing, and her words have stayed with me throughout my entire career. It also reminded me that other adults are always observing us wherever we are in the building.

This one small comment from this counselor encouraged me to keep doing what I was doing, and her words have stayed with me throughout my entire career.

Practical Wisdom for the Classroom

If you are going into your school at night or on the weekend, set a timer. Commit to spending a certain amount of time and not going over that time. This will help you to work efficiently and can prevent you from chatting too long with other teachers who are in the building.

Take Care of You

Being the best version of yourself is the most important thing you can do for your students. A well-rested, healthy, happy teacher is the most effective teacher. Once you have left for the day, create a transition routine. A transition routine might be something like, driving home while listening to something that brings you joy or changing your clothes when you get home and going for a short walk before you continue your evening. This will allow you to sleep better and keep you more balanced.

••• I USE A ROUTINE TO TRANSITION FROM WORK TO HOME.

PAUSE. REFLECT. ACT.

Erin's story demonstrates that we are always being observed by others: in our classrooms, out in the halls, and even on the playground.

- How do you communicate with your students in public?

- Who encourages you and compliments you?

- What will you do this week to support your growth as a teacher?

Write your responses to the prompts in a journal to further your reflection and to help you remember what you are learning. An online journal for your use is available on our companion website (resources.corwin.com/WeeklyWisdom). ●

27

GAIN TRUST THROUGH SHARING

Nicole Forinash
10 years

One big thing that I have learned in my career is to intentionally create relationships with every student, especially the hard-to-reach students. When you get to know your students, their interests, hobbies, and something about their lives, it allows them to open up to you. This is how you will see success in your classroom on more than one level. Relationships are important to every aspect of a child's success, and just as important for a teacher.

The hard-to-reach students are usually the ones that need to be shown more love and more compassion. They need to learn that you are someone they can trust

I had been at my current school for five years when a hurricane hit our state, and I was one of the unfortunate teachers who lost everything in the flood. Through the trauma, I decided to put my energy toward not only rebuilding but also communicating more openly with students who also lost everything. My students had never experienced loss like this before, and because I talked with them daily, they realized that I was in the same situation and they were able to open up and talk about their feelings. A lot of my students struggle with talking about their feelings because of their home lives, but this situation allowed us to be open, and, in turn, the students began to trust me a little more each day.

Take the time to talk to your students. Five minutes a day of open conversation is all it takes for a student to begin to trust you. Do not stress about conversations that cut into a reading or math block. The conversations that have taken place in my classroom have done more than allow students to trust and respect me; their academics have also shown growth due to the mutual trust.

Five minutes a day of open conversation is all it takes for a student to begin to trust you.

Practical Wisdom for the Classroom

I start off every day by having students write in their journals. They can share their thoughts with me or not, but this is their time to write about their feelings, or what they did the night before or over the weekend. This is their personal time of reflection, and it helps to focus their minds so they can be ready to focus on the school day.

Take Care of You

I will use my PERSONAL days and take a mental health day periodically. These days are meant to be used—so use them! I also participate in yoga, which helps clear my mind and stretch my body. It also helps me remember what is important in my life. My daughter and I enjoy baking together, and I take time to spend in the woods with my husband and daughter, connecting with nature. Your health, physical and mental, comes before anything else, and you need to make sure you are taking care of you!

●●● I TAKE CARE OF MY MIND AND MY BODY.

PAUSE. REFLECT. ACT.

Nicole used her experience of the flood to connect with her students. Because she was experiencing the same loss, they could see she also understood their pain.

- How do you gain your students' trust?

- What experiences do you have in common with your students?

- What will you do this week to support your growth as a teacher?

Write your responses to the prompts in a journal to further your reflection and to help you remember what you are learning. An online journal for your use is available on our companion website (resources.corwin.com/WeeklyWisdom). ●

REFLECTIONS

28 EXPECT THE UNEXPECTED

Pam King
16 years

During my first year with my own seventh-grade classroom, I coordinated a whole-class field trip to Boston. The highlight of the trip was a whale watch. The year had been challenging; I was a new teacher overwhelmed by my teaching assignment and overloaded with extra duties. I wanted to execute everything perfectly and spent hours micromanaging details for this trip and for my teaching in general.

When we arrived in Boston, it was a dreary, rainy New England morning, and I thought they might cancel our outing. No such luck. Out we went: four teachers, six parent chaperones, and eighty twelve-year-olds. Very few were prepared for the elements, and before long, they were freezing in soaked hoodies and T-shirts. The weather made for rough waters, and we were about an hour into the trip when the first child threw up. One turned into three, three turned into ten, and ten turned into fifty.

I am not lying when I tell you that almost every child was sick, as well as ALL SIX parent chaperones. The crew passed out sick bags, but other than that, they were no help. Somehow, the other three teachers and I cared for all of these kids—grabbing bags, wiping tears, holding them up at the railing, huddling together with them to keep them warm—all without getting sick. God gives teachers stomachs of steel.

When we arrived back on land, we all looked like we had gone to war. The next event was an IMAX movie, during which they all took a much needed, albeit expensive, nap. They started to muster their energy after that, as kids do, and we enjoyed the rest of our day visiting the aquarium and eating great food at Faneuil Hall. When we got back on the bus that night to head home, we were laughing about this field trip we would never forget. This wet, icky, sicky day completely changed my relationship with those kids. Having those moments together, in the mess, showed me it was our relationships and experience together that mattered. I wished that we had done the field trip earlier in the year, long before I had to say goodbye to them at the end of June.

I have never forgotten that trip or those students. And while I don't do the Boston trip every year, I do my best to create experiences where we are having fun together or sharing troubles together or solving problems together. When we all know we're in it together, it makes it much easier for all of us to do our part.

When we all know we're in it together, it makes it much easier for all of us to do our part.

Practical Wisdom for the Classroom

PICK YOUR BATTLES. When I first started teaching, I believed I needed complete control; I addressed every infraction. Many new teachers err on the side of too strict or too soft, and I was on the strict train. I regret that time and wish I had known better. In my attempts to "look like a teacher who had it all together," I ended up a teacher who created a space that likely limited learning. We have to allow kids to make mistakes, allow ourselves to make mistakes, so we can learn how to do that appropriately.

An effective classroom doesn't ignore distracting or inappropriate behaviors but redirects in the most subtle way possible. The train is moving; we don't want to let students hop off, or worse yet, we don't want to throw them off. We need to give them whatever it is they need in that moment, so we can all keep moving. The better you know the students, the easier time you will have figuring out what they need. Some need gentle and patient attention, some need a look that you mean business, some respond well to humor. Some may just need a quiet, "Are you doing okay today?" A question like that, rather than a reprimand, can change where things are going. You are approaching with concern over their well-being rather than negativity.

Take Care of You

Teachers are often asked to do more, stay later, and take more on, usually with no additional pay.

My advice for a new teacher is to avoid giving an automatic yes when asked to do additional work. Saying no is difficult, but essential. Someone once told me to prioritize what you *need* to do, what would be *nice* to do, and what is *nuts* to do!

••• I KNOW WHAT I NEED TO DO, AND I DO IT.

PAUSE. REFLECT. ACT.

We cannot control everything, even if we try. Pam's story, while overwhelming, allows us to see the humor in the day-to-day life of a teacher.

- What are you trying to control? How is that working for you?

- How do you know when to pick your battles with your students?

- What will you do this week to support your growth as a teacher?

Write your responses to the prompts in a journal to further your reflection and to help you remember what you are learning. An online journal for your use is available on our companion website (resources.corwin.com/WeeklyWisdom). ●

29 APOLOGIZE WHEN YOU MAKE A MISTAKE

Jaclyn Lekwa
8 years

I will never forget the first time I handled a physical student outburst when I taught fifth grade. During independent centers time, a student flipped a desk over and was outwardly very upset about something. I instantly called administration to remove the student from my class instead of taking the time to understand what had caused this outburst.

I thought I had failed this student by not taking the time to listen to him, and therefore I was no longer a person he could trust. When he came to school the next day, I pulled him aside privately and I apologized to him. I remember being shocked when he interrupted me to say he was also sorry for what had happened. I learned what an impact it leaves on our students when we also admit to our mistakes as adults and show them we also strive to be better.

Take the time to understand your students, and don't be afraid to humanize yourself with them. Being able to build a relationship with each individual student you serve is an important step in fostering a loving and respectful relationship between you and your students. Sometimes, an apology is what is needed. And in this case, my student was also able to apologize to me for his over-reactive behavior. We both learned.

I remember being shocked when he interrupted me to say he was also sorry for what had happened.

Practical Wisdom for the Classroom

Pick a handful of strategies that work for you to manage student behaviors, and stick to them. There are endless possibilities when it comes to using positive reinforcement, incentives, and consequences, and trying to incorporate too many strategies can cause confusion for the teacher and the students. Ultimately, relationships and getting to know your students as individuals provide the key to management. Not only does this connection build a tight sense of trust and community in the classroom, but it also helps teachers know when to anticipate challenging behaviors.

Take Care of You

I was fortunate enough to have a wonderful mentor teacher my first year who instilled the concept of managing work-life balance. She gave me two pieces of advice that I still use to this day. First, take advantage of each minute of the workday. If you have five minutes of free time, use that time to grade papers and stay up to date with your gradebook.

Second, make a weekly and daily to-do list. This strategy helped me map out all the tasks that needed to get done and everything else running through my mind.

••• I USE MY TIME WISELY.

PAUSE. REFLECT. ACT.

Jaclyn's story shares her feelings about not getting to the root cause of the situation before she reacted.

- Is there a student you owe an apology? How might apologizing change your relationship?
- What are some of your positive reinforcement strategies?
- What will you do this week to support your growth as a teacher?

Write your responses to the prompts in a journal to further your reflection and to help you remember what you are learning. An online journal for your use is available on our companion website (resources.corwin.com/WeeklyWisdom). ●

GIVE YOURSELF GRACE

Cassie Tabrizi
19 years

Teaching is one of the best and most fulfilling jobs in the world. That also makes it one of the hardest. Being a new teacher can make you feel like you are drowning. Drowning in paperwork, drowning in responsibilities, and drowning in to-do lists. When you are feeling overwhelmed, and like you can barely keep your head above water, remember to give yourself grace. Skip grading that one assignment, laugh at a lesson that went horribly wrong, or relieve yourself from the guilt that comes from feeling like you are always falling short. Newsflash: most of us feel like we are always falling short. You are trying your best and working as hard as you can. Things will get easier as you go. I promise.

Learning how to ask for help without feeling shame was the best thing I ever learned how to do. We are all in this together, and asking for help is a sign of strength, not weakness. Asking for help helped me see that I wasn't alone in a job that felt tough. It showed me that there were people ready and willing to help me. They empowered me so I could empower my students.

Being shown love and kindness when I asked for help led me to foster that same environment in my classroom. Our students can feel that same shame and embarrassment when asking for help. If we foster a loving and supportive environment, where asking for help is expected and reciprocated, we are setting our students up for so much more success in the long run.

Learning how to ask for help without feeling shame was the best thing I ever learned how to do.

Practical Wisdom for the Classroom

Try to plan a week ahead. This includes making copies and preparing any materials you might need for the week. If you can stay a week ahead, you won't be spending as much time scrambling to get your lesson going on the day of. You'll also save yourself the time of having to stay hours after contract time trying to play catch-up.

Take Care of You

Keep your favorite treat in your desk at all times. Don't share it with anybody! You can't control a lot of what happens at school, but you can control a few small bites of joy every day.

PAUSE. REFLECT. ACT.

Cassie's story helps us understand that when we learn a lesson, we also model that learning for our students.

- Where do you need help right now? Why aren't you asking for help? Who will you ask?

- What is the favorite treat you will keep in your desk?

- What will you do this week to support your growth as a teacher?

Write your responses to the prompts in a journal to further your reflection and to help you remember what you are learning. An online journal for your use is available on our companion website (resources.corwin.com/WeeklyWisdom). ●

CLOSING THE SCHOOL YEAR WITH INTENTION

CELEBRATE YOUR GROWTH

WEEKS 31–36

These last six weeks of school can go by so quickly you miss them. I remember my first years of teaching being such a blur. One minute you are moving at 1000 percent, and the next day all the students are gone, and you find yourself sitting in an empty room with a mess around you. The last six weeks are important because this is the time when you can assess how each of your students has grown over the year. It is also a time for your own self-assessment. It hasn't all been a struggle, has it? What are the moments of joy you experienced this year? Or what "you just can't make this up" experiences have you had this year?

The experienced teachers contributing to this "Closing the School Year With Intention" chapter will share how you can acknowledge your students publicly, see your success through their eyes, and find reasons to celebrate with them. These teachers encourage you to slow down so you can and see your full potential and be inspired for next year.

Schedule time each week to read and reflect on what is most useful to you, and write your insights in a personal journal, or use the online option on the companion (Visit the companion website at **resources.corwin.com/ WeeklyWisdom.**)

31

ACKNOWLEDGE STUDENTS PUBLICLY

Julia Poole
10 years

During the school year, my classroom would frequently host visitors: people from the district office, prospective families, teachers on an interview tour, or philanthropists eager to help combat educational injustice. Initially, these visits were disruptive to my students and my teaching because I thought the visitors might be judging my classroom.

To minimize this feeling, I decided to implement a process that included feedback from the visitors prior to their departure. The students and I created an adjective poster with words that we hoped described our classroom, words like *focused, engaged, courteous,* and *spirited.* Before a visitor exited the classroom, I'd ask if they would share their impressions either using words from the poster or providing their own impressions.

This feedback from our guests gave a clear message to my students that their good behavior was noticed. Instead of having guests just walk through silently observing, we now had a formal interaction and some closure to the visit. The recurrent exercise also helped calm my own nerves—as I was always hyper aware of what was going wrong in my classroom, especially with an audience present. Focusing on what was working in public helped me and my students acknowledge what others saw. After every guest visit, we celebrated and savored the good we were creating together each day.

A routine for publicly celebrating what you notice is going well is especially valuable at the end of the year. As a teacher, it is important to complement each student publicly and use those adjectives that relate to the values you have been teaching. I would often ask the principal or another teacher to come visit at the end of the year and notice the growth we'd made since September. You can never give too many compliments to your students!

After every guest visit, we celebrated and savored the good we were creating together each day.

Practical Wisdom for the Classroom

Ask your principal, "Who is one of the most effective teachers in this building?" Shadow that person. One of the best ways to become an excellent teacher is to witness excellence in your building. Here are five things to watch for.

1. How does the teacher greet students at the door? Notice how she stands, holds her shoulders, and gestures with her hands.

2. How does the teacher redirect students? Quietly? With humor? Through positive reframing?

3. What techniques does the teacher use to wrap up the class in the final two minutes of the lesson?

4. In what ways does the teacher reinforce a sense of belonging in the school community?

5. With whom does the teacher eat lunch, and in what ways does he reenergize between classes?

Take Care of You

Make a best friend at work who is as committed as you are to becoming an excellent teacher. Research from Gallup suggests that having a best friend at work makes you seven times more likely to be engaged. One of the ways to energize during the day is in the company of others. As Mr. Rogers would say, "Look for the helpers." They are in every school.

●●● I CHOOSE LIKE-MINDED FRIENDS TO KEEP MY SPIRITS UP.

PAUSE. REFLECT. ACT.

When someone enters our classroom space, we may feel judged. Julia created a way to include the students in a process that allowed them to share their good behavior with others.

- How do you prepare your students for visitors or observers?

- Who would you like to observe at your school?

- What will you do this week to support your growth as a teacher?

Write your responses to the prompts in a journal to further your reflection and to help you remember what you are learning. An online journal for your use is available on our companion website (resources.corwin.com/WeeklyWisdom). ●

32

INVITE YOUR STUDENTS TO GRADE YOU

Joan Vohl Hamilton
36 years

For the final twenty years of my career, I would ask my students to "grade" my class. This was the final assignment of the year: the final exam had been taken, and I asked them to complete this after all my grades had been submitted. The honest input of my students (because the input was always anonymous unless they chose to sign their names) helped me improve my teaching each year.

It took some courage for me to do this, but I'd been giving them feedback all year. Students are asked to provide honest feedback in college. Why not in eighth grade?

Indeed.

So, the students would brainstorm together the year's highlights—assignments and activities—and write them on the board. Then they would answer the following:

1. What, for you, was the favorite part of English class this year? Why?

2. What, for you, was the least favorite part of English class this year? Why?

3. What suggestions do you have for me to improve the class for next year's eighth graders? Please explain.

4. Is there anything else you would like to share with me?

Yes, there'd always be a few kids who were jerks, but most students gave thoughtful and honest answers. This input made me a better teacher.

> The honest input of my students would help me improve my teaching each year.

Practical Wisdom for the Classroom

This may seem counterintuitive, but OVER PREPARE. Expect technology to be unreliable, expect a fire drill, expect . . . whatever. If your main lesson runs short, you can roll into "what's next." If your class becomes disrupted, you know the goal that's most important for the day and can focus on it. Over preparing saves you time—again and again.

Take Care of You

I find my balance when I am focusing on my family. It is the best self-care I can give myself. While my daughter was growing up, I led her Girl Scout troop for nine years. I led a Destination Imagination creative problem-solving team for five years and was also a band parent. Was I busy? Yes! Was it worth it? Yes! I took the summer off from most of these volunteer gigs and focused completely on my family and my gardens. You, your mental health, and your outlook on life will all benefit when you vary outside-the-classroom experiences. My focus on my family made me a better teacher.

●●● **I AM WILLING TO HEAR WHAT MY STUDENTS HAVE TO SAY ABOUT MY TEACHING.**

PAUSE. REFLECT. ACT.

It takes courage to hear what your students have to say.

- What do you think of Joan's idea to have the students "grade" you? Will you try it?
- How can over preparing for classes save you time in the long run?
- What will you do this week to support your growth as a teacher?

Write your responses to the prompts in a journal to further your reflection and to help you remember what you are learning. An online journal for your use is available on our companion website (resources.corwin.com/WeeklyWisdom). ●

33 SEE YOUR SUCCESS THROUGH YOUR STUDENTS' EYES

Nancy Legan
45 years

The end of each school year is such a whirlwind, but I would never miss this important closing activity. I'd ask my students to write a letter to the students who would be in my class next year. I would put some ideas on the board to guide their letters: what to expect in this classroom, how they would describe me as a teacher, what they learned this year, how the new student would enjoy this grade, or anything they wanted to share.

The resulting products not only served as a welcoming activity for students in the next year but also provided me an opportunity to reflect on my practice at the end of the current school year. The students' recollections pointed out what they found valuable and enjoyable in my class. I could also look to see whether my goals for the year were embedded in their experiences.

In the teaching profession, a chance to improve is always available. Using the students' voices to guide our practice is invaluable. This activity allowed me to hear how they talked with other students about their experience of learning.

One of the common themes that often emerged was their description of me as a teacher who was *firm but fair.* I liked that my students saw me that way and that in the next year, my new class was introduced to me through my former students' eyes.

The students' recollections pointed out what they found valuable and enjoyable in my class.

Practical Wisdom for the Classroom

Compliment your students with phone calls to their parents. Keep a list of your calls, and find something positive to say about each student in your classroom. You can do this at any time of year, but it is especially valuable at the end of the school year when final grades and assessments might not always represent the growth you have seen in particular students. Your positive acknowledgment of progress goes a long way with your students and their parents.

Take Care of You

We all have our bad days, but make a sincere effort to verbalize the positive. When you stop and think about your day, there is always something that happens that can make you smile or even laugh. Celebrate those small moments. I always feel better when I shift my attitude.

●●● **I COMPLIMENT MY STUDENTS WITH PHONE CALLS TO THEIR PARENTS.**

PAUSE. REFLECT. ACT.

This approach of inviting students to write letters to next year's class gives us an insider view of what our students think about their classroom experience.

- What do you like about Nancy's story and closing activity?

- How can you stay positive when people around you are negative?

- What will you do this week to support your growth as a teacher?

Write your responses to the prompts in a journal to further your reflection and to help you remember what you are learning. An online journal for your use is available on our companion website (resources.corwin.com/WeeklyWisdom). ●

34 SLOW DOWN AND REFLECT

Tara M. Dexter

18 years

Entering into a new profession oftentimes brings an array of different feelings and emotions, which can range from joy to fear. That being said, if I could share anything with a novice teacher it would have to be the story of the *Tortoise and the Hare.* We enter into the workforce happily eager to begin a career; we have worked hard to learn how to teach, how to be effective, how to plan multifaceted lessons to ensure students meet academic standards. UDL (universal design for learning) lessons are carefully planned, and social and emotional skills are carefully tended to so that we reach and target *all* students.

Our zest for teaching and desire to make a difference in students' lives pushes us to plan it all out, get a jump start on the year, and go all in. But the same enthusiasm that fuels us to go-go-go full speed ahead can cause us to forget one thing. We forget about us. We are human beings and need to remember that sometimes fast is not best; sometimes taking time to reflect should take priority (both for our own mental health and for the benefit of our teaching).

The Tortoise didn't go as fast as the Hare. The Tortoise slowed down when needed, reflected on the race, and took time to think about which path to choose; the Hare was gung-ho, steadfast in his mindset and confident in his ability, yet somehow, in the end, he managed to lose the race. As you enter the teaching profession, don't lose sight of the importance of slowing down. Enjoy the journey, and reflect.

When reflecting—whether it be on how the day or the lessons went or on student achievements—you may realize there is an area of your teaching where you need some support. Don't be afraid to seek out the guidance of others. In this profession, you are NOT alone. Whatever it is that you are trying to work through, more than likely, someone else has already gone through something similar.

As you complete your school year, seek out resources by asking your mentor, a grade-level partner, another teacher, or the instructional coach for help. As uneasy as it may be to put yourself out there, you are forming relationships with colleagues during these moments. Having a support system is crucial to your growth as an educator. We all started out on an unknown path, and there are many people who are willing to help you navigate your journey.

These people are resources who will help you to master the craft of teaching; they will also help you recognize and cultivate an awareness of your own well-being, which is crucial to your career as an educator.

As you enter the teaching profession, don't lose sight of the importance of slowing down. Enjoy the journey, and reflect.

Practical Wisdom for the Classroom

Remember to set boundaries for your time. Make a list that contains "Do Now," "Can Do This Week," and "Can Do Next Week or Next Month." Set an alarm on your phone to alert you when to stop working for the night—and then GO HOME. Remember, students deserve the best version of you EVERY DAY. Your best version is not attainable if you are overworked and overtired!

Take Care of You

Every morning before work, I take my dog for a walk or a ride in the car. This helps me get ready for the day and brings me a sense of peace. Each night when I go home, I reflect on my day, and I make my list of things that need to get done the next day. But most of all, I spend quality time at the dinner table with my family. During this time, we sit and talk to each other and enjoy each other's company.

••• I ASK FOR HELP WHEN I NEED IT.

PAUSE. REFLECT. ACT.

The end of the school year can be overwhelming. There is so much to do and not a lot of time to do it.

- How does Tara's message support you in ending the year smoothly?

- What are your morning and evening self-care routines?

- What will you do this week to support your growth as a teacher?

Write your responses to the prompts in a journal to further your reflection and to help you remember what you are learning. An online journal for your use is available on our companion website (resources.corwin.com/WeeklyWisdom). ●

35

BE A LEADER

Megan Martens
11 years

Getting selected by my peers to be Teacher of the Year for my school led to significant positive growth in my teaching career. When I was chosen to be among the top five finalists for the county, I had the opportunity to become part of a fantastic group of teacher leaders who were selected to support other teachers in our county. The goal of the program was to uplift and inspire current teachers at all levels and to build teacher leaders throughout our district.

Because of this opportunity, I now see myself as a teacher leader. I understand now that there are many like-minded educators out there, and we all want to have a positive impact on our schools. Because of this experience, my role shifted to include supporting and mentoring other educators throughout the district, with other time still spent in the classroom teaching students.

As an educator, you are learning every day, whether it is your first year, tenth year, or thirtieth year. It is important to always be humble and ask for help when needed. Having a strong support system, whether from a mentor teacher, other instructional leaders, or other educators, is key to long-term success.

Because of this leadership opportunity, I now see myself as a teacher leader.

Practical Wisdom for the Classroom

Use volunteers to help you during the year and especially at the end of the school year. Volunteers are amazing resources to help you prepare materials for lessons or to set up materials. You would be surprised how many people are willing to help. Using volunteers also builds positive relationships among educators, families, and the community.

Take Care of You

You have to train yourself to leave the school day at school and make time for yourself outside of school. Do not let your school life take over your home life. I love to listen to inspirational podcasts, visit old churches, and take forest-bathing walks in the woods. All of these experiences give me a feeling of gratitude and support me in appreciating my life and the beauty around me. This is how I find and keep my balance.

●●● I HAVE A LIFE OUTSIDE OF SCHOOL.

PAUSE. REFLECT. ACT.

Beginning teachers can be leaders too. You may have experience in areas that can help your school. Don't be shy.

- What stands out to you in Megan's leadership message?

- How can you use volunteers to help you?

- What will you do this week to support your growth as a teacher?

Write your responses to the prompts in a journal to further your reflection and to help you remember what you are learning. An online journal for your use is available on our companion website (resources.corwin.com/WeeklyWisdom). ●

FIND REASONS
TO CELEBRATE

Mike Pelletier
23 years

A few years back, our school decided to change the schedule and get rid of the familiar seven-minute homeroom period. I admit the change had me feeling sentimental. Homeroom was one place a teacher could get to know students outside of the academic, "I grade your papers" context.

More than that, teachers had "followed" the same homeroom students from their first year all the way through senior year. In many ways, this allowed relationships to develop. Over the last year, I'd had a group of seniors whom I had gotten to know well over the previous four years. A friendly comment about the game last night to a first-year student walking into homeroom could (and in some cases did) lead to an ongoing four-year conversation about Boston sports.

We decided a party was necessary. What better party than a home-room breakfast party? We planned to celebrate on the last day of school. Every single student contributed something to make that breakfast special. There was music, a variety of caffeinated beverages, and all types of food, much of it homemade. Some of the food wasn't even breakfast food. Despite the fact that it was 7 a.m., I recall eating a shrimp and noodle dish that was one of the best things I've ever tasted. Remembering that morning makes me smile.

I think what I like most about that memory is that everyone did it together. Every single homeroom student showed up early that morning—the quiet kids, the loud kids, you know, all of them—and many of their friends as well. The kids socialized, laughed, and generally enjoyed each other. Though we were commemorating the end of an era with a simple party, in a larger way, we were showing each other the best of ourselves and what we can do and be. We can work together for a larger goal. We can make contributions that showcase our unique perspectives and experiences. We can appreciate the unique contributions of others. We can always find a reason to celebrate.

Though we were commemorating the end of an era with a simple party, in a larger way, we were showing each other the best of ourselves and what we can do and be.

Practical Wisdom for the Classroom

I'm not sure I've got any secrets for making the most of scarce time. But one thing that works for me is trying to complete one task before I go on to the next. There are so many different things that teachers need to do that it can be overwhelming. I find I'm more productive and effective when I give my full attention to one task until it's complete, rather than having lots of incomplete tasks "open" all at once.

Take Care of You

Wait, what? It's not a 24/7 job? For me, I take care of my mind and body by doing physical activity, like sports. Nothing changes my mood and attitude more quickly than running around for a while. It helps me find a way on Saturday to laugh at the thing that frustrated me on Friday.

••• I MOVE MY BODY TO CHANGE MY MOOD.

PAUSE. REFLECT. ACT.

Mike's story illustrates the importance of bringing our students together in celebration. Discovering milestones worth noting is one way a teacher can create a community of students.

- What is worth celebrating with your students?

- How does Mike's message of focusing on one task at a time resonate with you?

- What will you do this week to support your growth as a teacher?

Write your responses to the prompts in a journal to further your reflection and to help you remember what you are learning. An online journal for your use is available on our companion website (resources.corwin.com/WeeklyWisdom). ●

LOOKING BACK, LOOKING FORWARD

REFLECT AND PLAN

Closing Letter to Beginning Teachers

Dear Beginning Teachers,

You made it! We hope the weekly wisdom from these experienced teachers has guided you through the year in a supportive way. These teachers have served as mentors to help you to focus on your practical craft knowledge as well as your personal self-care. I hope their stories and messages offered the support you needed at the perfect time. You can learn more about each of these teachers on the companion website.

Even though these teachers represent different subject areas and grade levels and come from many different states and school districts, they have shared a common message for all teachers.

Three big ideas stood out to me.

1. **Relationships** matter—relationships with your students, your colleagues, the staff at the school, parents, and the community. A teacher is like an orchestra leader. We have to manage all the many

different instruments and bring them together to create that sweet music. When one section of the orchestra is out of tune, it influences all the others. You are a master of creation. Relationships with all the key players will support you in your role as a teacher.

2. **Routines** keep your classroom running smoothly. Planning every aspect of each student movement in your classroom is just as important as delivering your content. Using time-saving tips for managing paperwork frees up more of your time to talk to students. Responding to student behavior with caring and understanding lets students see you as a fair and consistent role model. In fact, if we don't have these "management" routines established and understood by our students, there is very little teaching and learning going on.

3. **Respect** for ourselves and our personal lives makes us better teachers. Intentionally scheduling time for friends, family, exercise, or anything that brings you personal satisfaction will give you the energy you need to experience the joy in your classroom. It will support your health to avoid burnout. And it will also help you to see that teaching can be a fulfilling career.

We never really know the influence we have on our students. Remember my story at the very beginning of this book ("Bloom Where You're Planted") when I was teaching in a portable classroom with a student who couldn't read? I never would have guessed that Billy M. would become a teacher!

Be a Ripple

Do you want to be a positive influence in the world?

First, get your own life in order. . . .

Your behavior influences others through a ripple effect.

A ripple effect works because everyone influences everyone else.

Powerful people are powerful influences.

~ Lao Tzu

As a teacher, YOU are a powerful influence on your students, their families, and the community. Thank you for choosing to be a teacher and for completing this year-long mentoring journey with us.

May your next year be filled with your own wisdom!

* Carol

Assess Your Year: What Did You Learn?

Take the time to complete the following short assessment and capture the wisdom that was meaningful to you.

1. **Review** ~ the four seasons opening pages.

   List any ideas that stand out to you as important messages to remember.

2. **Revisit** ~ your insights from the journal you kept this year.

   List any ideas that stand out to you as important messages to remember.

3. **Rethink** ~ your teaching practices.

Make inspired decisions for next year. List three things you will do differently.

Pay It Forward: Share Your Wisdom With Others!

You have learned so much this year! Thirty-six experienced teachers have taught you and mentored you, providing you with many new ideas and ways to enhance your classroom practice.

How will you share what you learned with other beginning teachers in your school or district?

Here are some ideas to get you started.

1. **Start a beginning teacher support group to share best practices!**

   If you have been reading the *Weekly Wisdom* book with other beginners, you may want to continue your journey next year. You can watch a video about how to organize your group agenda on the companion website.

2. **Read the book again next year with a teacher partner.**

   Find a teacher friend, a mentor, or another teacher at your school and do a one-to-one peer mentoring program with each other. Schedule coffee and conversation, phone calls, or in-person meetings, and just share ideas and do some problem solving together.

3. **Reach out to some legacy teachers (retired teachers) in your district for inspiration.**

   I believe legacy teachers have an abundance of wisdom to share with beginners; they also have the time to share! Ask your mentor or administrators how you can reach out to a wise teacher to get some mentoring for your next year.

4. **Review the resources on the Mentoring in Action website.**

   I have created a website with plenty of resources and videos for beginning teachers (mentoringinaction.com). Explore, share, and use the resources to refine your teaching practices.

5. **Write your own wisdom story and share it!**

   You are ready to share what you are learning with others. Use the *Weekly Wisdom* model in this book to share a story and what you learned, write a "management" tip that you absolutely love, and describe what you are doing for your self-care.

The goal of this book is to support you in learning and growing. When we started this journey at the beginning of the school year, I shared a quote from one of my mentors, Roland S. Barth.

I will end this book with his words.

> *The most powerful form of learning, the most sophisticated form of staff development, comes not from listening to the good words of others but from sharing what we know with others. . . .*
>
> *By reflecting on what we do, by giving it coherence, and by sharing and articulating our craft knowledge, we make meaning and learn.*
>
> ~ Roland S. Barth (1986)

Thank you for being willing to learn, to grow, and to share what you know with others. This is the most powerful form of teacher learning.

APPENDICES

APPENDIX A
OVERViEW OF COMPANiON WEBSiTE RESOURCES

This is a list of additional resources you will find on the companion website (resources.corwin.com/WeeklyWisdom).

Meet the Teachers Who Contributed to This Book

Take some time to learn more about the teachers who shared their wisdom with you (resources.corwin.com/WeeklyWisdom). You will notice they represent different grade levels, content areas, states, district sizes, and years of experience.

Bonus Wisdom

These teachers, whose stories and tips did not fit easily into the selected framework of the book, offer you more wisdom and suggestions for practices to integrate into your classroom and life (resources.corwin .com/WeeklyWisdom).

Weekly Wisdom Reflections: Online Journal

You may want to use the journal on the companion website to reflect on how each teacher's message is useful to you (resources.corwin .com/WeeklyWisdom). These reflections will also be helpful to document your growth as a teacher.

Weekly Wisdom Affirmation Posters (Printable)

There are four printable posters available (resources.corwin.com/Weekly Wisdom). A copy of these posters to remind you of the affirmations as you move through the four seasons of the school year.

Dedication Background Information: The Sean Duarte Story of a Beginning Teacher

Sean was a former student teacher who passed away suddenly at the beginning of his student teaching program. Learn more about Sean and his message to all of us (resources.corwin.com/WeeklyWisdom).

Mentoring in Action Resources

You will find free resources on my website (https://mentoringinaction .com/) to support mentors, novices, and all teachers in your school. My books are available through Corwin, and the courses are downloadable. A guide to these Mentoring in Action resources is available on the companion website (resources.corwin.com/WeeklyWisdom).

Introducing the Legacy Teacher Network

This is an idea I am inspired to share with all of you. Take a look at the concept, and see how retired teachers can support beginning teachers through mentoring conversations that promote well-being (resources .corwin.com/WeeklyWisdom).

Create a Circle of Light

Another way to support teachers is through a book study I created using *Teaching With Light: Ten Lessons for Finding Wisdom, Balance, and Inspiration.* Review the steps to creating your own circle (resources.corwin.com/WeeklyWisdom).

Maintaining a Life: Margaret Metzger's Message to Beginning Teachers

I read this article years ago and had the opportunity to write to the author when I was teaching a group of beginners. Her advice to my future teachers can be found on the companion website (resources.corwin.com/WeeklyWisdom).

The Art of Living: A Message From Carol

I offer you one last piece of wisdom to guide your journey (resources.corwin.com/WeeklyWisdom). Share this message with your students, so they may also learn from you that life is for living.

SEVEN WAYS TO SUPPORT BEGINNING TEACHERS USING THIS BOOK

1. **Give a Book to Your New Hires** ~ Collaborate with the Human Resources Department and school leaders and provide this book as a gift to all the teachers who are hired. Write a short personal note and place it in the book welcoming the teachers to the district and letting them know they are appreciated. Share the mentoring program schedule and other support systems the teachers can expect from your district.

2. **Create a Support Group for All New Teachers** ~ Connect with mentor leaders in the district and work together to schedule times when beginning teachers can get together and share ideas, ask questions, and solve problems collaboratively. Use the book as a guide for sharing. Novice teachers have wisdom too! Encourage them to share what they are learning.

3. **Organize a Book Study** ~ Use mentor leaders as facilitators for a book study where teachers of all stages and levels can come together to read the wisdom and discuss the ideas offered in the book. Meet 4 times a year using the "seasons" of the book to guide the discussion.

4. **Schedule Ten Minutes for Weekly Inspiration** ~ Integrate ten minutes each week as part of a department or school-wide effort to focus on the well-being of teachers. Use the book as content for sharing a story, a management tip, or advice on how to maintain balance.

5. **Enhance Mentoring Discussions** ~ Provide copies of the books for all your mentors and mentees and invite them to use the content as a guide to share their own stories and wisdom with each other.

6. **Collaborate With a Local College** ~ Student teachers can benefit from reading this wisdom before they begin student teaching. Share the book with faculty and invite them to use it in their teacher education courses. Include student teachers in the book study or support groups.

7. **Invite (Retired) Legacy Teachers to Mentor** ~ Learn more about my vision for a Legacy Teacher Network on the companion website. Legacy teachers are valuable resources who can support novice teachers beyond year one when mentoring is usually offered. The book is a guide for sharing wisdom and practical strategies to promote wellness.

REFERENCES

Barth, R. S. (1986). The principal and the profession of teaching. *The Elementary School Journal, 86*(4), 471–492. (Barth adapted his words from this published source, page 486.)

Klein, A. (2021, December 6). 1,500 Decisions a day (at least!): How teachers cope with a dizzying array of questions. *EducationWeek.* https://www.edweek.org/teaching-learning/1-500-decisions-a-day-at-least-how-teachers-cope-with-a-dizzying-array-of-questions/2021/12

Radford, C. P. (2021). *Teaching with light: Ten lessons for finding wisdom, balance, and inspiration.* Corwin.

Tzu, L. (1986). *The tao of leadership: Lao Tzu's Tao Te Ching adapted from a new age* (John Heider, Ed.). Humanics Pub Group.

Other Titles to Consider

A Mentoring Guide for Novice Teachers
SECOND EDITION

CAROL PELLETIER RADFORD

Foreword by Peter DeWitt

THE FIRST YEARS MATTER:
Becoming an Effective Teacher

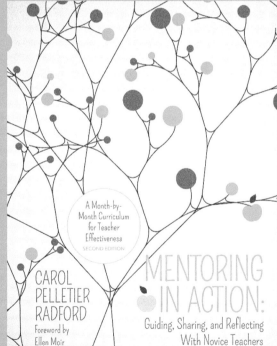

A Month-by-Month Curriculum for Teacher Effectiveness
SECOND EDITION

CAROL PELLETIER RADFORD

Foreword by Ellen Moir

MENTORING IN ACTION:
Guiding, Sharing, and Reflecting With Novice Teachers

TEACHING with LIGHT

TEN LESSONS FOR FINDING WISDOM, BALANCE, & INSPIRATION

CAROL PELLETIER RADFORD

CORWIN

A SAGE Publishing Company

Helping educators make the greatest impact

CORWIN HAS ONE MISSION: to enhance education through intentional professional learning.

We build long-term relationships with our authors, educators, clients, and associations who partner with us to develop and continuously improve the best evidence-based practices that establish and support lifelong learning.